JERM
STR
TH

Farm Hall

By Katherine Moar

Performed at Jermyn Street Theatre, London,
9 March – 8 April 2023

Farm Hall

by Katherine Moar

CAST

BAGGE	Archie Backhouse
WEIZSÄCKER	Daniel Boyd
HEISENBERG	Alan Cox
DIEBNER	Julius D'Silva
HAHN	Forbes Masson
VON LAUE	David Yelland

PRODUCTION TEAM

Director	Stephen Unwin
Set and Costume Designer	Ceci Calf
Lighting Designer	Ben Ormerod
Sound Designer	John Leonard
Casting Director	Ginny Schiller CDG
Assistant Director	Millie Gaston
Production Manager	Lucy Mewis-Mckerrow
Stage Manager	Daisy Francis-Bryden
Assistant Stage Manager	Fae Hochgemuth
Costume Supervisor	Lauren Savill
Lighting Programmer	Jodie Underwood
Set Construction	Overflow Events Ltd.
Production Technician	Tom McCreadie
PR	David Burns

Thanks

Jonathan Kydd, Corin Buckeridge, Iris Ibañez Rojas, The Watermill Theatre, Royal Central School of Speech and Drama, Mountview, National Theatre

Special thanks to our former Artistic Director and Executive Producer Tom Littler.

Cast

BAGGE | Archie Backhouse

Theatre credits include: *The Wonderful World of Dissocia* (Stratford East); *Telethon* (TalkShow); *Hunger* (Arcola); *The Listening Room* (Crowded Room/ UK tour); *There is a Field* (Synergy/Theatre503); *The Outsider* (Print Room at the Coronet); *The Gap in the Light* (New Diorama).

Television credits include: *The Sandman* (Netflix); *Save Me* (World Productions/Sky Atlantic).

Archie is an actor and deviser, he worked with theatre maker Christopher Green on his show *No Show* (The Yard) and is an associate artist with Complicité.

Archie trained at The Royal Central School of Speech and Drama.

WEIZSÄCKER | Daniel Boyd

Theatre credits include: *Private Peaceful* (Nottingham Playhouse/UK tour); *Great Expectations* (West Yorkshire Playhouse); *Bad Jews* (Theatre Royal Bath/UK tour); *Oppenheimer* (RSC/West End); *The Shoemaker's Holiday* (Royal Shakespeare Company); *4000 Miles* (Theatre Royal Bath/The Print Room, Evening Standard Theatre Award nomination); *Romeo and Juliet* (Headlong).

Television credits include: *The Toys that Built America* (History Channel); *Brave New World* (NBC); *Holby City*, *Horizon – Einstein*, *Silk* (BBC); *Misfits* (Clerkenwell Films); *Richard II: The Hollow Crown* (Neal Street Productions).

Film credits include: *On Chesil Beach*; *Tiger House.*

Daniel trained at the Royal Conservatoire of Scotland.

HEISENBERG | Alan Cox

For Jermyn Street Theatre: *Love All*, *Barefoot in the Park.*

Theatre credits include: *Two Ukrainian Plays*, *But It Still Goes On*, *Cornelius*, *Chu Chin Chow*, *Atman* (Finborough); *Uncle Vanya*, *Longing*, *The Rubenstein Kiss* (Hampstead); *Hamlet* (Shakespeare Theatre Company, Washington); *The Divided Laing* (Arcola); *City Stories* (St James Studio); *Kingmaker* (Arts); *Playing with Grown Ups* (Brits Off Broadway); *The Caretaker* (Adelaide Festival/US tour); *The Tempest* (Jericho House); *Blok/Eko*, *Hurts Given and Received*, *Found in the Ground*, *The Fence* (The Wrestling School); *Behind the Eye* (Cincinnati Playhouse); *50 Hour Improvathon* (Hoxton Hall); *Much Ado About Nothing* (Chester Performs);

Orwell: A Celebration (Trafalgar Studios); *Frost/Nixon* (US tour); *Natural Selection* (Theatre503); *Passion Play* (Goodman Theatre, Chicago); *Translations* (Manhattan Theatre Club); *The Creeper* (Playhouse); *The Earthly Paradise* (Almeida); *John Bull's Other Island* (Lyric, Belfast); *The Flu Season* (Gate); *The Importance of Being Earnest* (Theatre Royal Haymarket); *The Duchess of Malfi* (Salisbury Playhouse); *Three Sisters* (Birmingham Rep); *An Enemy of the People, Wild Oats, Absolute Hell, The Seagull* (National Theatre); *The Lady's Not for Burning, On the Razzle* (Chichester Festival Theatre); *Strange Interlude* (Duke of York's); and several productions for the Royal Shakespeare Company.

Television credits include: *New Amsterdam* (NBC); *The Good Wife* (CBS); *Lucan, A Voyage Around My Father, Housewife 49* (ITV); *The Odyssey* (Hallmark).

Film credits include: *Magic Mike's Last Dance*; *The Speed of Thought*; *Not Only But Always*; *Act Naturally*; *Ladies in Lavender*; *The Waterfalls of Slunj*; *Cor Blimey*; *The Auteur Theory*; *Contagion*; *Mrs. Dalloway*; *An Awfully Big Adventure*; *Young Sherlock Holmes*.

DIEBNER | Julius D'Silva

Theatre credits include: *& Juliet* (Shaftesbury); *What's New Pussycat?* (Birmingham Rep); *The Producers* (Manchester Royal Exchange); *The Cherry Orchard* (Bristol Old Vic/Manchester Royal Exchange); *Strictly Ballroom* (West Yorkshire Playhouse/Toronto); *Made in Dagenham* (Adelphi); *Eternal Love* (Shakespeare's Globe/English Touring Theatre/UK tour); *Anne Boleyn* (Shakespeare's Globe/English Touring Theatre); *Macbeth* (Shakespeare's Globe); *Oliver!* (Theatre Royal Drury Lane); *Aristo* (Chichester Festival Theatre); *Histories Ensemble* (Olivier Awards for Best Company Performance, Best Revival, Best Design), *Henry IV Parts 1 & 2, Henry V, Henry VI Part 1, Henry VI Part 2, Henry VI Part 3, Richard III, Dog in the Manger, Tamar's Revenge, House of Desires, Pedro, the Great Pretender* (Royal Shakespeare Company); *Great Expectations* (Royal Shakespeare Company/Cheek by Jowl); *The Wax King* (HMP Pentonville); *The Tempest* (Edinburgh Festival); *Measure for Measure* (Rome); *Vergil, Caesar* (Oxford Playhouse); *Bouncers* (Burton Taylor); *Richard II* (Ludow Festival).

Television credits include: *Bridgerton, The Crown* (Netflix); *The Ten Commandments* (Hallmark); *How We Used To Live: Spanish Armada* (Yorkshire Television); *Highlander* (Gaumont Television).

Film credits include: *Notes on a Scandal*; *Full Circle*; *Endgame*.

HAHN | Forbes Masson

Theatre credits include: *The Taxidermist's Daughter* (Chichester Festival Theatre); *The Magician's Elephant, The Boy in the Dress, Macbeth, Hamlet, The Comedy of Errors, Twelfth Night, The Histories, As You Like It, Romeo and Juliet, The Taming of the Shrew* (Royal Shakespeare Company); *Summer and Smoke* (Almeida/Duke of York's); *Little Shop of Horrors* (Regent's Park Open Air Theatre); *Travesties* (Menier Chocolate Factory/ Apollo); *Mr Foote's Other Leg* (Hampstead/Theatre Royal Haymarket); *Doctor Faustus* (Duke of York's); *Macbeth, Richard II, The Ruling Class* (Trafalgar Studios/Jamie Lloyd Productions); *Big Fish* (The Other Palace); *King Lear* (Liverpool Everyman/Young Vic/Headlong); *The Lion, the Witch and the Wardrobe* (Kensington Gardens); *Bartholomew Fair, The Merry Wives of Windsor, Boudica* (Shakespeare's Globe); *Dumbstruck* (Lyric Hammersmith); *Art, The Breathing House* (Lyceum Edinburgh); *Life of Stuff* (Donmar Warehouse); *The Trick is to Keep Breathing, The Real World* (Tron).

Television credits include: *The Crown* (Netflix); *Royal Mob* (History); *As You Like It* (CBeebies/Globe); *Irvine Welsh's Crime* (BritBox); *Shetland, Monarch of the Glen, Rab C Nesbitt, City Lights, Hamish Macbeth* (BBC); *Taggart* (STV); *Catastrophe* (Channel 4).

Radio credits include: *Doctor Who – Wages of Time, Doctor Who – Girl Interrupted, Jago and Lightfoot* (Big Finish); *The Rise of the Nazis, Macbeth, The Tempest, Nuremberg, Doors* (BBC); *Raj* (Audible).

Films credits include: *The Road Dance; Gypsy Woman.*

Writing credits include: *Stiff* (Tron/Lyceum); *The High Life* (BBC); *Victor and Barry* (Edinburgh Festival/Donmar Warehouse/Sydney Opera House); *Mince* (Dundee Rep); *At Home with Feste* (Royal Shakespeare Company); *Jack and the Beanstalk, Cinderella, Weans in the Wood, Snow White* (Tron); *Crackers* (Belgrade, Coventry).

Forbes is an associate artist with the RSC and National Theatre of Scotland.

VON LAUE | David Yelland

For Jermyn Street Theatre: *All Our Children.*

Theatre credits include: *The Habit of Art, Phaedra, Britannica, Hamlet, John Gabriel Borkman, The Shoemaker's Holiday, Summer, Major Barbara* (National Theatre); *A Patriot for Me* (Haymarket/Los Angeles); *Time and the Conways, The Merchant of Venice, Rumours, The Circle, For King and Country,* A *Marvellous Year for Plums* (Chichester Festival Theatre); *An Ideal Husband* (Haymarket/Broadway); *Waste, The Seagull, King Lear* (Old Vic);

The Misanthrope, *Major Barbara* (Piccadilly); *Cuckoos* (Gate/Barbican); *As You Like It* (Bath/US tour); *Deathtrap* (Garrick); *The Deep Blue Sea* (Haymarket); *The Rules of the Game*, *The Jew of Malta* (Almeida); *The Prime of Miss Jean Brodie* (Strand); *The Seagull*, *Tosca's Kiss* (Orange Tree); *The Importance of Being Earnest* (Old Vic); *Richard III* (Savoy, Clarence Derwent Award); *God Only Knows* (Vaudeville); *Life x3* (Savoy); *Henry IV* (Donmar Warehouse); *Man and Boy* (Duchess); *Troilus and Cressida* (Edinburgh Festival/Royal Shakespeare Company); *For Services Rendered*, *Single Spies* (The Watermill); *Nicholas Nickleby* (Chichester Festival Theatre/Gielgud/Prince of Wales/Toronto); *Mrs Warren's Profession* (Theatre Royal Bath/UK tour/West End); *Henry IV* (Theatre Royal Bath); *Uncle Vanya* (Print Room); *An Ideal Husband*, *Mrs Warren's Profession* (Gate, Dublin); *Taken at Midnight* (Chichester Festival Theatre/Haymarket); *A Winter's Tale* (Shakespeare's Globe); *Witness for the Prosecution* (London County Hall).

Television credits include: *David Copperfield*; *Star Quality*; *The Bretts*; *Rumpole of the Bailey*; *Waking the Dead*; *The Inspector Lynley Mysteries*; *The Line of Beauty*; *Rocketman*; *Poirot*; *Love Soup*; *Midsomer Murders*; *Spooks*; *Foyle's War*; *EastEnders*; *Law & Order UK*; *Bones*; *The Crown*; *Reg*; *Father Brown*; *Endeavour*; *The Diplomat*.

Film credits include: *Happy End*; *Hunter Killer*; *Coriolanus*; *Private Peaceful*; *Chariots of Fire*.

Creative Team

WRITER | Katherine Moar

Katherine studied history at the University of Edinburgh and Darwin College, Cambridge. She is currently studying for a PhD at King's College London, analysing public perceptions of Winston Churchill from the First World War to 2020. *Farm Hall* is her first play.

DIRECTOR | Stephen Unwin

Stephen Unwin is an award-winning British theatre and opera director. He has directed almost 100 professional productions and worked with many well-established actors and singers, as well as developing the careers of many younger ones.

In the 1980s he worked at the Almeida, the Traverse in Edinburgh, in repertoire theatre and at the National Theatre Studio. 1993, he founded English Touring Theatre, for whom he directed more than 30 productions of classical and new plays, many of which transferred to London. In 2008, he became Artistic Director of the new Rose Theatre in Kingston, which he ran until January 2014. He has directed more than 20 operas.

Stephen has taught in conservatoires and universities in Britain and America and written 10 books on theatre and drama, including *Poor Naked Wretches*, a study of Shakespeare's working people (Reaktion 2022). He has also written five original plays (*All Our Children* was premiered at Jermyn Street Theatre in 2017, and staged in New York in 2019) and numerous translations.

Stephen is a campaigner for the rights and dignities of learning-disabled people and is completing a new book on the representation of learning disabilities in culture and society.

www.stephenunwin.uk
Twitter: @RoseUnwin

SET AND COSTUME DESIGNER | Ceci Calf

For Jermyn Street Theatre: *Orlando*, *Rocky Road*, *One Million Tiny Plays About Britain* (also Watermill).

Theatre credits (as Designer) include: *Under the Black Rock* (Arcola); *A Skull in Connemara* (Dailes Teātris, Latvia); *Not Now* (Finborough); *Othello* (Watermill); *Twelfth Night* (Kew Gardens); *Warrior Queens* (Sadler's Wells); *Tapped* (Theatre503); *The Mozart Question* (Barn, Cirencester); *To Have and*

To Hold (Hope); *Yes So I Said Yes*, *How to Survive an Apocalypse*, *Not Quite Jerusalem*, *The Wind of Heaven* (Finborough); *Five Green Bottles*, *Tithonus* R&D (Sherman); *Cheer*, *Mydidae* (The Other Room); *The Cut* (LAMDA/Lion and Unicorn); *Yellow Moon* (LAMDA).

Theatre credits (as Associate Designer) include: *Anything Is Possible If You Think About It Hard Enough* (Southwark Playhouse).

LIGHTING DESIGNER | Ben Ormerod

For Jermyn Street Theatre: *Saviour*, *Footfalls* and *Rockaby* (also Theatre Royal Bath).

Theatre credits include: *The Beekeeper of Aleppo*, *Assassins* (Nottingham Playhouse); *Joyce's Women* (Abbey); *The Sex Party* (Menier Chocolate Factory); *A Christmas Carol*, *The Duchess of Malfi*, *Long Day's Journey into Night*, *The Oresteia*, *Hamlet*, *King Lear* (Citizens, Glasgow); *Don Juan* (Perth); *The Sunset Limited* (Boulevard); *Prism* (Birmingham Rep/UK tour); *The Scent of Roses*, *The Duchess of Malfi*, *A Number* (Royal Lyceum, Edinburgh); *Uncle Vanya*, *Loyalty* (Hampstead); *All's Well That Ends Well* (Sam Wanamaker Playhouse); *A Midsummer Night's Dream* (Regent's Park Open Air Theatre); *Zorro* (West End/US/Netherlands/Japan); *Mrs Henderson Presents* (Bath/West End/Canada).

Opera credits include: *Die Tote Stadt*, *The Ring Cycle*, *Tristan und Isolde* (Longborough Festival); *The Elixir of Love* (Into Opera); *La traviata* (Danish National Opera); *Jeanna D'arc au Bûcher* (Academia Santa Cecilia, Rome); *Falstaff*, *Il trovatore* (Scottish Opera); *La traviata* (English National Opera); *The Nutcracker*, *Les Noces* (Ballet Geneva); *Frame of View* (Cedar Lake Contemporary Ballet/Theater Augsburg).

SOUND DESIGNER | John Leonard

For Jermyn Street Theatre: *All Our Children*, *Told Look Younger.*

Theatre credits include: *As You Like It* (@sohoplace); *The Sex Party* (Menier Chocolate Factory); *The Snail House*, *Night Mother*, *Wolf Cub*, *Cell Mates*, *The Meeting*, *Stevie* (Hampstead); *The Dresser* (Theatre Royal Bath/UK tour); *The Stepmother*, *8 Hotels* (Minerva, Chichester); *Prism* (Hampstead/UK tour); *Blithe Spirit* (Theatre Royal Bath/UK tour/West End); *Bloody Difficult Women* (Hammersmith Riverside/Edinburgh Festival); *Consent*, *Cocktail Sticks* (National Theatre/West End); *My Name is Lucy Barton* (Bridge/Friedman, New York); *Uncle Vanya* (Bath Theatre Royal); *Charlotte & Theodore*, *In Praise of Love* (Ustinov, Bath); *Long Day's Journey into Night* (Bristol Old Vic/West End/New York/Los Angeles); *Hand To God* (Vaudeville); *McQueen* (St. James/West End); *Firebird, Mr. Foote's Other Leg* (Hampstead/West End); *Ghosts* (Almeida/West End/Harvey, Brooklyn).

Sound Designer John Leonard has worked for most of the major theatre companies in the UK and extensively in London's West End, Broadway and on national and international tours. He is the author of a renowned textbook on theatre sound, winner of Drama Desk and Sound Designer of the Year awards and is a Fellow of the Guildhall School of Music and Drama, an Honorary Fellow of The Hong Kong Academy of Performing Arts and a Companion of The Liverpool Institute of Performing Arts.

CASTING DIRECTOR | Ginny Schiller CDG

Ginny has been an in-house casting director for the RSC, Chichester Festival Theatre, Rose Theatre Kingston, English Touring Theatre and Soho Theatre and has worked closely with Bath Theatre Royal and Ustinov Studio for the last decade. She has cast extensively for the West End and touring circuit as well as for the Almeida, Arcola, Birmingham Rep, Bolton Octagon, Bristol Old Vic, Cambridge Arts, Charing Cross Theatre, Clwyd Theatr Cyrmu, Frantic Assembly, Hampstead Theatre, Headlong, Jermyn Street, Leicester Curve, Liverpool Everyman and Playhouse, Lyric Theatre Belfast, Menier Chocolate Factory, Northampton Royal & Derngate, Nottingham Playhouse, Oxford Playhouse, Plymouth Theatre Royal and Drum, Regent's Park Open Air Theatre, Shakespeare's Globe, Shared Experience, Sheffield Crucible, Traverse Edinburgh, West Yorkshire Playhouse, Wilton's Music Hall, Young Vic and Yvonne Arnaud Guildford. She has also worked on many television, film and radio productions, including the BBC Radio 4 series *Nuremberg* and *Nazis: The Road to Power*. Some recent productions include *Noises Off* with Felicity Kendal and Matthew Kelly, Deborah Warner's *The Tempest* at the Ustinov Studio, *The Starry Messenger* at the Wyndham's, *The Best Exotic Marigold Hotel* directed by Lucy Bailey, *Bad Jews* at the Arts Theatre and *The Snail House* for Richard Eyre at Hampstead Theatre.

ASSISTANT DIRECTOR | Millie Gaston

For Jermyn Street Theatre: *Shake the City*, *Monarchy*.

Theatre credits (as Writer) include: *At the End of the Road*, *Shake the City* (Leeds Playhouse); *The Robin and the Holly Tree* (Slunglow); *Hon3y92* (Northern Broadsides); *The Happy Warrior* (York Army Museum/ Harrogate); *Erin* (Harrogate).

Theatre credits (as Actor) include: *Ruby and the Vinyl*, *A Christmas Carol* (John Godber Company); *The Accident Did Not Take Place* (York Theatre Royal); *Crown Prince: Part of a* (Wakefield Theatre Royal); *Snowflake* (Malvern Theatres); *Three Emos* (regional tour/UK tour), *The Remarkable Tale of Dorothy McKaill* (Hull New Theatre); *Hon3y92* (Northern Broadsides); *MT Fest* (The Other Palace); *Th'Importance of Bein Earnest* (Drayton Arms); *King Lear* (Here To There Productions).

Millie trained at the Manchester School of Theatre. She is the Johnston Creative Associate at Jermyn Street Theatre.

STAGE MANAGER | Daisy Francis-Bryden

For Jermyn Street Theatre: *Orlando*, *Footfalls* and *Rockaby* (also Theatre Royal Bath).

Theatre credits include: *Who's Holiday* (HOME/Southwark Playhouse); *UK Drill Project* (Barbican Pit); *Horse-Play* (Riverside Studios); *The Man in the Moon* (St Paul's Church/Belcombe Court); *Originals: Live at Riverside Studios* (Riverside Studios); *The Night Woman* (The Other Palace); *On the Line* (London schools tour); *GirlPlay* (Camden People's Theatre); *The Duration* (Omnibus).

Daisy Francis-Bryden is a freelance Production and Stage Manager. Since graduating in 2021, they have worked on a variety of productions across London within the Stage Management department, including Stage Manager on Book, and Assistant Stage Manager.

a small theatre with big stories

WHO WE ARE

Jermyn Street Theatre is a unique theatre in the heart of the West End: a home to remarkable artists and plays, performed in the most intimate and welcoming of surroundings. World-class, household-name playwrights, directors and actors work here alongside people just taking their first steps in professional theatre. It is a crucible for multigenerational talent.

The programme includes outstanding new plays, rare revivals, new versions of European classics, and high-quality musicals, alongside one-off musical and literary events. We collaborate with theatres across the world, and our productions have transferred to the West End and Broadway. Recently, our pioneering online work and theatre-on-film has been enjoyed across the world.

A registered charity No. 1186940, Jermyn Street Theatre was founded in 1994 with no core funding from government or the Arts Council. Since then, the theatre has survived and thrived thanks to a mixture of earned income from box office sales and the generous support of individual patrons and trusts and foundations. In 2017, we became a producing theatre, the smallest in London's West End. Around 60% of our income comes from box office sales, and the rest in charitable support and private funding.

★★★★★
❝ **Unerringly directed ... no one in this tiny theatre dared breathe.** ❞

The Observer

From top: Jack Reitman in Thrill Me: The Leopold & Loeb Story, 2022; Jennifer Kirby in The Massive Tragedy of Madame Bovary, 2022. Photos by Steve Gregson.

★★★★★

OVER THE YEARS

1930s
During the 1930s, the basement of 16b Jermyn Street was home to the glamorous Monseigneur Restaurant and Club.

early **1990s**

1994
The staff changing rooms were transformed into a theatre by Howard Jameson and Penny Horner (who continue to serve as Chair of the Board and Executive Director today) in the early 1990s and Jermyn Street Theatre staged its first production in August 1994.

1995
Neil Marcus became the first Artistic Director in 1995 and secured Lottery funding for the venue; producer Chris Grady also made a major contribution to the theatre's development.

late **1990s**
In 1995, HRH Princess Michael of Kent became the theatre's Patron and David Babani, subsequently the Artistic Director of the Menier Chocolate Factory, took over as Artistic Director until 2001. Later Artistic Directors included Gene David Kirk and Anthony Biggs.

2012
The theatre won the Stage Award for Fringe Theatre of the Year.

2017
Tom Littler restructured the theatre to become a full-time producing house.

2020
Our audiences and supporters helped us survive the damaging impacts of the Covid-19 lockdowns and we were able to produce a season of largely digital work, including the award-winning *15 Heroines* with Digital Theatre +.

2021
We won the Stage Award for Fringe Theatre of the Year for a second time. Artistic Director Tom Littler and Executive Director Penny Horner were recognised in The Stage 100.

2022
We won a Critics' Circle Award for *Exceptional Theatre-Making During Lockdown* and an OffWestEnd Award for our Artistic Director.

Stella Powell-Jones and David Doyle succeeded Tom Littler as Artistic Director and Executive Producer respectively, working alongside Executive Director Penny Horner to form a management team of three.

 **support us**

> **" I recently became a Patron of Jermyn Street Theatre, as I believe passionately in the work it is doing. It would be wonderful if you could contribute. "**
>
> *Sir Michael Gambon*

Become a Friend of the theatre and enjoy a range of exclusive benefits. Join one of our four tiers of Friends with names inspired by *The Tempest* from just £50 a year.

Lifeboat Friends

Our **Lifeboat Friends** are the heart of Jermyn Street Theatre. Their support keeps us going. Rewards include priority booking to ensure they can get the best seats in the house.

The Miranda Club

Members of the **Miranda Club** enjoy all the benefits of the Ariel Club, and they enjoy a closer relationship with the theatre.

The Ariel Club

Members of the **Ariel Club** enjoy exclusive access to the theatre and our team. As well as the priority booking and Friends Nights enjoyed by Lifeboat Friends, **Ariel Club** members also enjoy a range of other benefits.

The Director's Circle

The Director's Circle is an exclusive inner circle of our biggest donors. They are invited to every press night and enjoy regular informal contact with our Artistic Director and team. They are the first to hear our plans and often act as a valuable sounding board. We are proud to call them our friends.

We only have 70 seats which makes attending our theatre a magical experience but even if we sell every seat, we still need to raise more funds.

Michael Gambon, Sinéad Cusack, Richard Griffiths, David Warner, Joely Richardson, Danny Lee Wynter, Rosalie Craig, Trevor Nunn, Adjoa Andoh, David Suchet, Tuppence Middleton, Martina Laird, Gemma Whelan, Eileen Atkins, Jimmy Akingbola and many more have starred at the theatre.

But even more importantly, hundreds of young actors and writers have started out here.

If you think you could help support our theatre, then please visit www.jermynstreettheatre.co.uk/friends/

Jermyn Street Theatre is a Registered Charity No. 1186940. 60% of our income comes from box office sales and the remaining 40% comes from charitable donations. That means we need your help.

our friends

The Ariel Club

Richard Alexander
David Barnard
Derek Baum
Martin Bishop
Dmitry Bosky
Katie Bradford
Nigel Britten
Christopher Brown
Donald Campbell
James Carroll
Ted Craig
Jeanette Culver
Valerie Dias
Shomit Dutta
Lucy Fleming
Anthony Gabriel
Carol Gallagher
Roger Gaynham
Paul Guinery
Debbie Guthrie
Diana Halfnight
Julie Harries
Andrew Hughes
Margaret Karliner
Keith Macdonald
Vivien Macmillan-Smith
Kate & John Peck
Adrian Platt
A J P Powell
Oliver Prenn
Martin Sanderson
Andrew WG Savage
Carolyn Shapiro
Nigel Silby
Bernard Silverman
Anthony Skyrme
Philip Somervail
Robert Swift
Gary Trimby
Lavinia Webb
Ann White
Ian Williams
John Wise

The Miranda Club

Anonymous
Anthony Ashplant
Geraldine Baxter
Gyles & Michèle
  Brandreth
Anthony Cardew
Tim Cribb
Sylvia de Bertodano
Janie Dee
Anne Dunlop
Robyn Durie
Maureen Elton
Nora Franglen
Robert & Pirjo Gardiner
Mary Godwin
Louise Greenberg
Ros & Alan Haigh
Phyllis Huvos
Frank Irish
Marta Kinally
Yvonne Koenig
Hilary King
Jane Mennie
Charles Paine
John & Terry Pearson
Iain Reid
Martin Shenfield
Carol Shephard-Blandy
Jenny Sheridan
Brian Smith
Frank Southern
Dana-Leigh Strauss
Mark Tantam
Paul Taylor
Brian & Esme Tyers
Jatinder Verma

Director's Circle

Anonymous
Judith Burnley
Philip Carne MBE &
  Christine Carne
Jocelyn Abbey & Tom
  Carney
Colin Clark RIP
Lynette & Robert Craig
Flora Fraser
Charles Glanville &
  James Hogan
Crawford & Mary Harris
Judith Johnstone
Ros & Duncan McMillan
Leslie & Peter MacLeod-
  Miller
James L. Simon
Marjorie Simonds-Gooding
Peter Soros & Electra
  Toub
Melanie Vere Nicoll
Robert Westlake & Marit
  Mohn

FARM HALL

Katherine Moar

*For my parents, Todd,
and Stephen Unwin*

.

'The story of Farm Hall is another complete play in itself.'

Michael Frayn
in his postscript to *Copenhagen*

Summary

Summer 1945. Hitler is dead. Germany is defeated. The war in the Pacific rages on.

In England, six of Germany's foremost scientists are detained following their capture by Allied forces. They are Hitler's Uranium Club, the men tasked with producing an atomic bomb for the Nazis.

Stowed safely in Farm Hall, a stately home nestled in a quiet corner of the Cambridgeshire countryside, these 'guests' of His Majesty are forced to entertain themselves. Removed from the chaos of war and convinced of their scientific superiority, they while away the hours playing chess, restoring a broken piano, and rehearsing an all-male amateur production of Noël Coward's *Blithe Spirit*.

But the war and the world cannot be shut out forever. The guests' tranquil summer is shattered by the revelation that the unthinkable has occurred, that the Americans have succeeded where the Germans have failed, that the United States has not only built an atomic bomb, but has used one against Japan...

During their seven-month detainment, unbeknownst to its occupants, almost every inch of Farm Hall was bugged. The guests' recorded conversations were translated, transcribed and, finally, in 1992, declassified and published as *The Farm Hall Transcripts*. This play is inspired by *The Farm Hall Transcripts* and by true events that occurred at Farm Hall between July 1945 and January 1946.

6

Characters

VON LAUE, *late sixties. An open objector to Nazism. Played
no role in Hitler's Uranium Club. Won the Nobel Prize for
Physics in 1914 for the discovery of the diffraction of X-rays
by crystals*

DIEBNER, *early forties. The head of Hitler's Uranium Club
when it was under the control of the Army Ordnance Office.
Nazi Party member*

HEISENBERG, *early forties. Replaced Kurt Diebner as the
symbolic leader of Hitler's Uranium Club when the army
ceded control to the Reich Research Council. He won the
Nobel Prize in 1932 for 'the creation of quantum mechanics'*

WEIZSÄCKER, *early thirties. Heisenberg's close friend and
colleague. Member of the prominent Weizsäcker family.
His father served as State Secretary at the Foreign Office of
Nazi Germany from 1938 to 1943, and as its Ambassador to
the Holy See from 1943 to 1945. His younger brother would
serve as President of Germany between 1984 and 1994*

BAGGE, *early thirties. Heisenberg's former student. Nazi Party
member. According to Heisenberg, Bagge came from a
'proletarian family'*

HAHN, *early sixties. Discovered nuclear fission, the process
that makes an atomic bomb possible. He received the 1944
Nobel Prize for Chemistry for this discovery. Anti-Nazi*

Note on Play

The Uranverein or 'Uranium Club' was the name given to the project to research nuclear technology, including nuclear weapons and nuclear reactors, in Nazi Germany during the Second World War. Broadly, there were two streams of activity. The first was led by Kurt Diebner and administered by the Army Ordnance Office. When it became clear that the Uranverein would not make a decisive contribution to ending the war, the army ceded control of the project to the Reich Research Council and Werner Heisenberg.

This text went to press before the end of rehearsals and so may differ slightly from the play as performed.

Prologue

May 1945. Somewhere in Germany.

A telephone rings. VON LAUE *moves from darkness into the
light and picks up the telephone. He places the receiver to his ear.*

VON LAUE. Hello? Yes, my darling, it's me. It's Max.

I was about to leave but then – can you guess who has shown
up? It's Samuel Goudsmit. Remember him? The Dutchman.
It seems he's working with the Americans.

Listen to me, Magda. He wants me to leave now and go with
him. Do you understand? I won't be coming home.

You'll be all right. You will, my darling. You will. This is the
American zone. Nothing bad will –

I don't know where. America, perhaps. England.

I'll be fine. I won't be alone. It seems Sam's rounding up all
the physicists left in Germany.

I need to go now, Magda. I'm so sorry. I love you. I'll be
with you as soon as I can.

VON LAUE *hangs up the phone.*

ACT ONE

Scene One

July 1945. Godmanchester, Cambridgeshire, England.

The warmly, if shabbily, decorated interior of Farm Hall.
The guests are rehearsing a production of Noël Coward's
Blithe Spirit.

WEIZSÄCKER *is directing,* DIEBNER *(reluctantly) is*
Charles, BAGGE *(struggling) is Ruth.* HEISENBERG *and*
VON LAUE *are watching the rehearsal.* HAHN *is busily*
copying out later scenes of the play onto loose sheets of paper
from their only hard copy of the script.

DIEBNER *(as Charles).* 'I haven't forgotten Elvira. I remember
her very distinctly indeed. I remember how fascinating she
was, and how maddening. I remember her gay charm when
she had achieved her own way and her extreme acidity when
she didn't. I remember her physical attractiveness, which
was tremendous, and her spiritual integrity, which was nil.'

HAHN *chuckles.*

WEIZSÄCKER *(admonishingly).* Hahn.

BAGGE *(as Ruth; the script millimetres from his face).* 'Was
she more physically attractive than I am?'

WEIZSÄCKER. Eyes up, Bagge.

BAGGE *(staring wide-eyed at* DIEBNER). 'Was she more
physically attractive than I am?'

DIEBNER. 'That's a tiresome question, dear, and fully deserves
the wrong answer.'

HEISENBERG *(under his breath).* That was the wrong answer.

WEIZSÄCKER *(pleadingly).* Heisenberg.

BAGGE. 'You really are very sweet.'

DIEBNER. 'Thank you.'

BAGGE. 'And a little naive, too.'

DIEBNER. 'Why?'

BAGGE. 'Because you imagine that I mind about Elvira being more physically attractive than I am.'

DIEBNER. 'I should have thought that any woman would mind – if it were true. Or perhaps I'm old fashioned in my view of female psychology.'

BAGGE. 'Not exactly old-fashioned, darling, just a bit di-didactic.'

Beat.

What does that mean? 'Didactic'?

WEIZSÄCKER. Oh, Bagge.

BAGGE. I'm sorry, but what does it mean?

HEISENBERG. What does it mean, Weizsäcker?

WEIZSÄCKER. It means, *it means…*

DIEBNER. It means?

HEISENBERG. It's like patronising, Bagge. *Herablassend.*

BAGGE. Use it in a sentence.

HEISENBERG. 'Professor Hahn is a clever man and an accomplished chemist, but his teaching style is somewhat didactic.'

HEISENBERG *squeezes* HAHN*'s shoulder, and* HAHN *pats his hand, laughing.*

VON LAUE. What do you know about his teaching style? You were never his student.

HEISENBERG. It was a joke.

VON LAUE. Do you want to know what they say about you, professor?

HEISENBERG. Certainly not.

HAHN. He's only teasing, Von Laue.

VON LAUE. I don't like to see it.

WEIZSÄCKER. It's well known that the cleverest men don't make the best teachers. Look at Einstein – disorganised, boring.

Shall we continue?

BAGGE (*confidently now*). 'Not exactly old-fashioned, darling, just a bit didactic.'

DIEBNER (*dispassionately*). 'I love you, my love.'

Silence.

WEIZSÄCKER. Do you? Come, doctor. I know your own romantic life has been historically limited, but please. Imagine. This is your wife.

DIEBNER. No.

WEIZSÄCKER. *Please.*

DIEBNER. No, I didn't sleep well. I need a glass of water.

WEIZSÄCKER. No.

HAHN. I'll get it.

WEIZSÄCKER. We're in the middle of a rehearsal.

DIEBNER. I want to read.

WEIZSÄCKER. Read what? *The Most Complete Field Guide to the Mushrooms and Toadstools of Britain and Ireland*, again?

DIEBNER. Toadstools are more interesting than this nonsense. Hopeless husbands and their miserable wives. Ghosts. Where's the substance?

HEISENBERG. I do find it strange that anyone could enjoy this sort of thing in the middle of a war. Actors prancing about onstage in Shaftesbury Avenue while the bombs rain down on their heads. What if the theatre was hit?

BAGGE. Shouldn't we be doing Goethe or something?

WEIZSÄCKER. No, it's important that we imbibe Anglo-Saxon culture if we're to become English.

VON LAUE. Are we becoming English?

WEIZSÄCKER. Wouldn't it be lovely?

VON LAUE. Do I have a choice?

WEIZSÄCKER. Less than a month out of Germany and he's already talking about choices. Of course, you have a choice, Von Laue, that is the great benefit of the Allied victory, but choose wisely. The alternative might be... you know...

HEISENBERG. If the Allies wanted us dead, we'd be dead. Take it as a compliment. We've been collected and protected because we are a sought-after commodity.

BAGGE. So no Goethe?

WEIZSÄCKER. There wasn't any Goethe in the pile.

VON LAUE. That is a shame.

WEIZSÄCKER. Come, professor, are you ready to play? Madame Arcati?

VON LAUE. Doctors Bagge and Diebner could do with some Goethe in my opinion. *Faust*, hm?

BAGGE. What does that mean?

DIEBNER (*quietly*). Ignore him. He only opens his mouth to argue.

WEIZSÄCKER (*to* VON LAUE). What can I say to convince you?

VON LAUE. Nothing. It's too silly.

HEISENBERG. You never know, you might enjoy it.

VON LAUE. I don't think it advisable to give in to Doctor Weizsäcker's every demand. I can't believe we've already resorted to dictatorship.

HAHN. Well, you know what they say. Home comforts.

HEISENBERG. We need to wean ourselves off tyranny.

WEIZSÄCKER. Let's do the seance now. Hahn, do you have the pages?

HAHN. Almost done.

WEIZSÄCKER (*in* VON LAUE's *ear*). 'Well, Madame Arcati – the time is drawing near!'

Scene Two

A few days later. HEISENBERG, WEIZSÄCKER *and* BAGGE. HEISENBERG *is reading.*

WEIZSÄCKER. So, Ringo Kid leaps from the top of the carriage –

BAGGE (*correcting him*). The stagecoach.

WEIZSÄCKER. The stagecoach. He leaps from the top of the stagecoach onto the first set of horses – there are three sets, three pairs of horses – and then onto the second, and then onto the third.

BAGGE. Did John Wayne really do that?

WEIZSÄCKER. Of course. And the Red Indians have guns too.

HEISENBERG (*without looking up from his book*). How did the Indians get the guns?

WEIZSÄCKER. Hatfield checks his gun and realises that he has just one bullet left. And he twists the thing, the carriage, or the gauge or whatever, so that the next bullet he fires will be that bullet. And by this point he knows it's hopeless, he knows that they're going to be captured and scalped by the Indians. And Mrs Mallory is cowering in the corner, praying. And slowly, Hatfield raises his gun to her head –

BAGGE. Why?

WEIZSÄCKER. Because he knows it will be better for her to have a quick clean death than be put through God-knows-what

by the Indians. But then, suddenly, there's a gunshot and
Hatfield slowly lowers his gun because *he's* been shot.

BAGGE. By who? Is he dead?

WEIZSÄCKER. By an Indian and wait. In the distance, you
hear this trumpeting noise, and you're not sure if it's real or
in Mrs Mallory's imagination, but then –

BAGGE. It's the cavalry!

WEIZSÄCKER. And the Indians run for it! And the stagecoach
draws to a halt, and Ringo Kid yanks the door open to check
that everyone's all right, and he sees that they've all gathered
around Hatfield, who's bleeding, and Hatfield says something
like 'if you see your father…' to Mrs Mallory, and then he
just dies.

BAGGE. And the baby?

WEIZSÄCKER. With the prostitute.

BAGGE. And then?

WEIZSÄCKER. And then – wait, do you want me to tell you
now or save it for later?

BAGGE. Better save it.

HEISENBERG. Thank God.

WEIZSÄCKER. You loved that film.

HEISENBERG. No, I didn't.

BAGGE. When did you see it?

HEISENBERG. '39. We were in Michigan for a conference.

BAGGE. Oh, I'm jealous. American films are brilliant.

WEIZSÄCKER. I'll do *Gone with the Wind* next.

HEISENBERG. Are they brilliant?

WEIZSÄCKER. Yes.

HEISENBERG. Better than ours?

WEIZSÄCKER. Yes.

HEISENBERG. Better than Lang?

WEIZSÄCKER. Yes. Especially since he went to America.

BAGGE. Thank God the cavalry arrive in time.

WEIZSÄCKER. Like art imitating life.

BAGGE. What do you mean?

WEIZSÄCKER. That's what's happened, hasn't it? In the war.

BAGGE. How is the war like *Stagecoach*?

WEIZSÄCKER. Well, we, the Germans, are the Red Indians.

BAGGE. Okay.

WEIZSÄCKER. Noble. Ancient. On the warpath.

BAGGE. All right.

WEIZSÄCKER. And Hatfield is the British. Steeped in tradition, genteel, but slightly... tired, shall we say. That leaves America. The cavalry. New, brash, late to the scene, but not too late to save the day, to save the stagecoach, to save Europe! Mrs Mallory, the prostitute, et cetera represent Europe in this clever analogy. France can be the prostitute.

BAGGE. What happens to the Indians after they are defeated?

WEIZSÄCKER. They become American.

Pause.

BAGGE. Did you mean it, then, when you said you wouldn't mind becoming English?

WEIZSÄCKER. I did. Does that shock you?

BAGGE. No.

WEIZSÄCKER. You're a good German boy, Bagge.

BAGGE. And what are you?

WEIZSÄCKER. A citizen of the world. I belong nowhere and to nothing.

HEISENBERG. That's sad.

WEIZSÄCKER. It's not. It's the best gift my rich parents ever gave me.

BAGGE. So you wouldn't care if we never went home?

WEIZSÄCKER. I would care for your sake, and for
Heisenberg's. I wouldn't like it that you were sad. But
Germany doesn't mean very much to me.

HEISENBERG. That's not true.

WEIZSÄCKER. It is.

HEISENBERG. Sometimes I think you just say things.

WEIZSÄCKER (*coyly*). Do I?

HEISENBERG. Yes. Because you like how they sound coming
out of your mouth.

Pause.

WEIZSÄCKER. What will you do, Bagge? When we're
released. Where will you go?

BAGGE. I'm not sure.

WEIZSÄCKER. Germany?

BAGGE. What future do I have there?

WEIZSÄCKER. A bright one. Heisenberg and I will look after
you.

BAGGE. Everyone will say 'Party man! Party man!' I'd rather
go to America and forget.

Beat.

Before we left, Wirtz and Bopp buried four grams of radium
below an oak tree with a broken branch. They plan to go
back for it. They will be rich.

HEISENBERG. Lucky them.

WEIZSÄCKER. Döpel went to Russia. Perhaps we missed
a trick.

BAGGE (*horrified*). What?

WEIZSÄCKER. He will be a king!

Pause.

What about you, Heisenberg? What are your plans?

HEISENBERG. Germany, of course.

BAGGE. It won't be like it was.

HEISENBERG. Maybe not right away. It will be up to us to put it back together.

WEIZSÄCKER. What about Britain or America? Diebner is thinking about going to Argentina.

BAGGE. Do they have uranium in Argentina?

WEIZSÄCKER. I don't know.

HEISENBERG. No. If any of our American or British or Argentinian colleagues want to learn about the uranium problem, then I'd be glad to host them in my laboratory in Germany.

BAGGE. Didn't the Americans come after you before the war?

HEISENBERG. Yes, at that same conference in 1939. Sam Goudsmit asked me to stay.

BAGGE. And you said no?

HEISENBERG. Obviously.

Pause.

BAGGE. I feel very sorry for him.

WEIZSÄCKER. Sam?

BAGGE. Yes.

HEISENBERG. It's a terrible thing.

BAGGE (*to* HEISENBERG). Did he… Was he very angry with you?

HEISENBERG. Yes.

BAGGE. I remember the picture you had of the two of you, on your desk, all through the war.

WEIZSÄCKER. He'll come round.

HEISENBERG. I don't think so.

WEIZSÄCKER. What more could you have done?

HEISENBERG. I could have pulled his parents off the train.

Silence.

WEIZSÄCKER. How different things would have been if you had gone to America. Bagge and I would have been in charge!

BAGGE. I have no desire to be in charge. I just want to do my work, by myself, with no one to bother me. And no more politics.

WEIZSÄCKER. What about Russia, Heisenberg?

HEISENBERG. Certainly not.

WEIZSÄCKER. 'Certainly not'!

HEISENBERG. There are conditions under which I might work outside Germany, but never in Russia.

WEIZSÄCKER. What conditions?

BAGGE. A nice, fat salary.

HEISENBERG. It's not about a fat salary, but there does have to be money available. And I'd need access to a cyclotron.

WEIZSÄCKER. If the Russians offered you your very own cyclotron, would you work for them?

HEISENBERG. Only if there were nothing else available. I would much rather work in Germany, then, I suppose, America, then Britain. Russia comes in a distant last. But if every other nation were to turn me away...

WEIZSÄCKER. They wouldn't. I have no doubt that you will be the prettiest princess at the post-war party. All the handsome young men will be clamouring for your attention. It's the Russians I feel bad for. They will have the most miserable crop of German scientists to pick from.

HEISENBERG. If they've got Döpel, they might not need anyone else.

WEIZSÄCKER. He isn't that good. What if Stalin got down on bended knee and kissed your feet?

HEISENBERG. That would likely turn me off.

WEIZSÄCKER. Oh, you are too cruel! What if he took both your hands in his, clasped your sweaty, interlocked fingers to his chest and, in floods of tears, promised you all the uranium in the Congo?

HEISENBERG. And all the tea in China?

WEIZSÄCKER. And all the tea in China, and all the heavy water in Norway.

HEISENBERG. That's tempting. And the world's largest cyclotron?

WEIZSÄCKER. Da, Professor Heisenberg, da.

HEISENBERG. I will think about it, Comrade Stalin. I wouldn't like to fill my dance card too early in the evening.

They all laugh.

Pause.

BAGGE. Do you think they're listening?

WEIZSÄCKER. What do you mean?

BAGGE. Are they recording us?

HEISENBERG. Why?

BAGGE. To find out about our work, learn our secrets.

WEIZSÄCKER. What secrets, Bagge? I don't think they care about your girl in Baden-Baden.

BAGGE. Weizsäcker!

They all look up at the ceiling.

HEISENBERG. I think you're safe. The Brits don't understand the real Gestapo methods. They're a bit old-fashioned in that respect.

Scene Three

Early morning. DIEBNER is reading alone, HAHN appears in the doorway.

HAHN. Good morning, Diebner.

DIEBNER. Good morning, professor.

HAHN. There's a cat in the garden.

DIEBNER. That's nice.

HAHN. Climbed all over my lap.

DIEBNER. I don't like cats.

HAHN. Ah.

> *Pause.*

> Reading?

DIEBNER. Yes.

HAHN. Why are you always reading? That's not a criticism. I admire you for it. I don't have the concentration.

DIEBNER. It passes the time.

HAHN. And what are you reading today?

> DIEBNER *holds up the cover of the book.* HAHN *reads the title –*

> *Gulliver's Travels.* Is it good?

DIEBNER. Not really.

> *Silence.* HAHN *looks closely at* DIEBNER, *who has gone back to reading his book.*

HAHN. I worry that you're lonely.

DIEBNER. You shouldn't worry about me. Why do you say that?

HAHN. Well, Weizsäcker and Bagge are close. And they worship Heisenberg. Von Laue and I are the old guard. You're rather isolated.

DIEBNER. Ostracised might be a better word, but it is to be expected.

HAHN. I'll speak to the others.

DIEBNER. There's no need.

HAHN. I will. It's not fair for them to leave you out, just because –

DIEBNER. I'd rather you didn't. I don't need to be liked.

HAHN. It's not about needing to be liked, but we should try to get along.

DIEBNER. Why? We aren't friends.

HAHN. We're colleagues.

DIEBNER. Yes, but we didn't get on before, why should we get on now?

HAHN. We get on.

DIEBNER. You tolerate me, very kindly. Von Laue won't look at me, Bagge avoids me. Heisenberg and Weizsäcker belittle me.

HAHN. They don't –

DIEBNER. They do. Weizsäcker does. Primarily, it seems, because I'm an experimental not a theoretical physicist.

HAHN. Schoolboy snobbery. It's not real.

Pause.

We shouldn't fight amongst ourselves. Who knows how long we might be here?

DIEBNER *goes back to reading his book.*

What do you have planned for the day?

DIEBNER. Nothing. I might change seats in a moment.

HAHN. Not more amateur dramatics?

DIEBNER. Certainly not.

HAHN. And have you heard the good news?

DIEBNER. Are we going home?

HAHN. Not that good. We're getting a piano.

DIEBNER. Why?

HAHN. It's a present. For good behaviour.

DIEBNER. When?

HAHN. Rittner didn't say, but soon, I imagine.

DIEBNER. Can you play the piano?

HAHN. Not really. Can you?

DIEBNER. No. Can any of us?

HAHN. Heisenberg is a beautiful player. I assume Weizsäcker can. He asked for it.

DIEBNER. The piano?

HAHN. Yes.

DIEBNER. Weizsäcker is very good at getting what he wants.

HAHN. Being the son of a diplomat…

VON LAUE *enters*.

Hello, Von Laue.

VON LAUE. Good morning, Hahn.

DIEBNER. Good morning, professor.

VON LAUE (*hesitantly*). Yes, good morning.

HAHN. Guess what?

VON LAUE. We're going home?

HAHN. We're getting a piano!

VON LAUE. Says who?

HAHN. Major Rittner.

VON LAUE. But I don't want a piano.

HAHN. Oh, it will be fun.

VON LAUE. I want Monopoly. What's the point of being in a democratic country if I can't play Monopoly?

HAHN. Ask Rittner.

VON LAUE. I have.

DIEBNER. Ask Weizsäcker to ask Rittner.

VON LAUE *storms out,* HEISENBERG *passes him in the doorway.*

HEISENBERG. Morning, Hahn. Morning, Diebner.

HAHN. Good morning, Heisenberg.

DIEBNER. Good morning.

HAHN. Von Laue's upset because we're getting a piano and he wanted Monopoly.

HEISENBERG. He should ask Rittner.

HAHN. He has.

HEISENBERG (*to* HAHN). Chess?

HAHN. Why not?

HEISENBERG. I'll get it.

HEISENBERG *leaves. From the corridor we hear* BAGGE *say 'Good morning, Heisenberg', and* HEISENBERG *reply 'Good morning, Bagge'.*

BAGGE *enters.*

BAGGE. Good morning, Diebner. Good morning, Hahn.

HAHN *and* DIEBNER. Good morning, Bagge.

BAGGE. The professor is very upset about something. I passed him on the stairs.

DIEBNER. He wanted Monopoly, but we're getting a piano instead.

BAGGE. If he wants Monopoly, he should –

HAHN *and* DIEBNER. Ask Rittner.

HAHN. He has.

BAGGE. A piano, though! That's exciting. I'm so bored. I've counted all the windows, stairs, and doorknobs in the house and classified every plant in the garden. I've buttoned and unbuttoned and rebuttoned my buttons. What else can I do?

HEISENBERG *returns with the chess set*.

What's that?

HEISENBERG. Chess.

BAGGE. Winner stays on?

DIEBNER. Can I play?

HEISENBERG. I think there's another set in the drawing room.

DIEBNER. Bagge, if I can find another set, will you play?

BAGGE *does not respond*.

Bagge?

BAGGE. All right.

DIEBNER *leaves*.

(*To* HEISENBERG *and* HAHN.) Switch with me.

HAHN. What?

BAGGE. One of you switch with me.

HAHN. Bagge.

HEISENBERG. No.

BAGGE. Switch with me.

HAHN. Why?

BAGGE. Because… Switch with me. Heisenberg, switch with me.

HEISENBERG. I want to play with Hahn.

BAGGE. You can, you can. Just let me play one game with Hahn, you play with Diebner, and then I'll leave, and you can play with Hahn.

HAHN. Play with Diebner, Bagge.

BAGGE. No. I'd rather not play at all.

HEISENBERG (*to* HAHN). White or black?

BAGGE *leaves*.

HAHN. Black.

DIEBNER *returns*.

DIEBNER. I couldn't find chess, but I've got backgammon.

Beat.

Where's Bagge?

HAHN. I'm not sure.

BAGGE *and* WEIZSÄCKER *enter*.

WEIZSÄCKER. Morning, all.

HAHN *and* HEISENBERG. Good morning, Weizsäcker.

WEIZSÄCKER. Have you heard the good news?

HAHN *and* HEISENBERG. Yes.

WEIZSÄCKER. We're getting a piano!

DIEBNER (*to* BAGGE). Are we playing?

BAGGE. Did you find another set?

DIEBNER. No, but I've got backgammon.

BAGGE. I don't know how to play backgammon. I'll play cards with Weizsäcker.

DIEBNER. What are you playing?

WEIZSÄCKER. Beggar-My-Neighbour.

DIEBNER. Can I play?

WEIZSÄCKER. It's sort of a two-person game. Sorry, Diebner.

BAGGE. Yes, sorry, Diebner.

HAHN (*to* DIEBNER). Winner stays on?

Scene Four

HAHN, VON LAUE, HEISENBERG *and* DIEBNER.
HEISENBERG *is giving a lecture.*

HEISENBERG. During their ascent, the individual globules
expand in size –

DIEBNER. Hang on, hang on. 'Expand in size'?

HEISENBERG. Yes.

DIEBNER. 'Expand in size'? You haven't established the
original size of the globules yet. What's the critical radius?

HEISENBERG. Well –

DIEBNER. Presumably, the original size of each globule is
dependent on both the depth and on the size of the fibre that
spawned that globule?

HEISENBERG. Yes.

DIEBNER. That would have been helpful to know.

HEISENBERG. But you know that. I know that. Why do I need
to say what we both already know?

HAHN. Remember, Von Laue? The constant bickering, the
constant undermining of one's colleagues in one's youth?

HEISENBERG. We aren't bickering –

VON LAUE. – I never bickered –

HEISENBERG. – perhaps Diebner is undermining.

DIEBNER. I am not undermining anyone. I'm merely
following the train of your thoughts, or struggling to follow,
I should say.

HEISENBERG. I move quickly, Diebner. Try to keep up.

DIEBNER. Too quickly. You are liable to make mistakes.

HEISENBERG. I have not made a mistake.

DIEBNER. Not yet. How much do the globules expand by?

HEISENBERG. It depends on the length of the journey. If the
fibres were ten to twenty micrometres in diameter, say, and the

container was ten centimetres in height, the globules would
reach a diameter of... close to one millimetre at their peak.

DIEBNER. So a factor of about one million in volume.

HEISENBERG. Yes. So, the globules rise –

DIEBNER. – reach the surface of the liquid and rupture.

HEISENBERG. Yes. Because of gravity.

DIEBNER. By way of buoyancy.

HEISENBERG. Yes.

DIEBNER. Yes.

HAHN. Think what the two of you might accomplish if you
worked together. Cooperation, not competition.

HEISENBERG. I think it unadvisable.

DIEBNER. It would be a bloodbath.

HAHN. You shouldn't be ruled by pride and jealousy.

HEISENBERG. Which of us is pride and which is jealousy?

DIEBNER. What about in the absence of gravity?

HEISENBERG. What?

DIEBNER. In the absence of gravity, would there be no
effervescence?

HEISENBERG. No, the CO_2 globules would still form, but
they wouldn't be able to rise. They'd remain pinned, with no
forces to detach them from their nucleation sites. The
globules would grow larger and larger inside the container
and, eventually, would replace the liquid. The container
would overflow.

DIEBNER. Fine.

HEISENBERG. Say, that a tenth of a litre of the liquid has been
poured into the second container, we can estimate that
approximately nought point seven litres of gaseous carbon
dioxide must escape for equilibrium to be regained. How
much effervescence does this involve? We can divide the

volume of the gaseous CO_2 in the second container, by the volume of an average globule, about five hundred micrometres in diameter, to get…

DIEBNER. Eleven million globules.

HEISENBERG. Yes.

DIEBNER. Critical thickness?

HEISENBERG. About one hundred nanometres.

DIEBNER. One-ten-thousandth of a millimetre.

HEISENBERG. In layman's terms, yes.

HAHN. Now, now, boys.

VON LAUE. What is all this, anyway? These numbers, these diagrams. It isn't any nuclear physics I recognise.

HAHN. I challenged them to work together on a new problem.

HEISENBERG. 'Méthode Champenoise.'

DIEBNER. How they put the bubbles in champagne.

Scene Five

HAHN *and* VON LAUE. HAHN *is fixing a broken piano with a large red bow on top;* VON LAUE *is aimlessly flicking through a book.*

HAHN. Pass me that, will you?

VON LAUE. What?

HAHN. That.

VON LAUE. This?

HAHN. Yes.

VON LAUE *hands it to him with great effort.*

Thank you.

HAHN *disappears behind the piano.*

Damn.

HAHN *pops back up, a piece of broken piano in his hand.*

VON LAUE. Oh, dear.

HAHN. I shouldn't've done that.

VON LAUE. No.

Pause.

HAHN. Will you help?

VON LAUE. Shouldn't those who asked for the broken piano, fix the broken piano?

HAHN. Those who asked for the broken piano are young. They want to do great work that makes them miserable, not menial work that will make them happy.

Pause.

What d'you think of Diebner?

VON LAUE. Why do you ask?

HAHN. I'm curious.

VON LAUE. I think you know the answer.

HAHN. You don't like him.

VON LAUE. What is there to like?

HAHN. And Bagge?

VON LAUE. Bagge has the good grace to act ashamed, at the very least. Diebner wears what he's done as a badge of honour. He expects us to be impressed.

HAHN. I don't think he does.

VON LAUE. He's very proud.

HAHN. I don't think he is.

Pause.

I think if you were kinder to them, more civil, it might make things easier for the rest of us. It's selfish of me to ask, I know, but –

VON LAUE. I'm sorry, Hahn, but I don't think I'm physically capable of that.

HAHN *sighs and continues to work diligently on the piano. The large red bow continually gets in his way.*

HAHN. Here, take this.

HAHN *throws the bow to* VON LAUE.

VON LAUE *misses, picks it up, and reads the card affixed to it.*

VON LAUE. 'Dear all, happy 27th July. Sorry it's a bit battered. I assume, given your smattering of Nobel Prizes, that this will not pose too much of a problem. Yours, Major T. H. Rittner.'

HAHN. I like Rittner. He's funny.

VON LAUE *tuts.*

You don't like him either?

VON LAUE. He's English.

HAHN. So?

VON LAUE. We're German.

HAHN. So? He's not the enemy, Von Laue. He's our host.

VON LAUE. He's our jailer.

HAHN. He's a very amiable jailer, and this is a very comfortable jail. If I had known prison was like this, I would have given up chemistry long ago and turned to a life of unsuccessful crime. Four-course dinners, brandy, chess, books, a piano –

VON LAUE. A broken piano.

HAHN. Yes, well, it won't be broken for much longer. Please help, Von Laue, I can't do it without you. It's no fun to work alone.

VON LAUE. Oh, all right. If only to end your incessant badgering.

HAHN. Here, you untangle these strings.

VON LAUE. To think, I was once director of my own institute.

HAHN. And you will be again! For now, I will make you Director of the Institute for Piano Strings.

VON LAUE. What are you?

HAHN. Director of the Institute for Indiscriminate Bits of Wood.

They lapse into a contented silence.

Throughout the following conversation, they continue to work on the piano.

Do you think Rittner is married?

VON LAUE. He wears a wedding ring.

HAHN. I can't imagine him out of uniform. I picture him eating in uniform, sleeping in uniform, marrying in uniform, playing with his children in uniform.

VON LAUE. You think he has children?

HAHN. Oh, yes. Three strapping boys. The spitting image of their father.

VON LAUE. I think girls. Two girls. He was so kind to that nurse in Versailles, remember? I wouldn't be at all surprised if he had a daughter her age.

Pause.

What about his wife?

HAHN. Oh, a formidable woman. Rittner may be soft on the inside, but he's hard on the outside. I think his wife is the same.

VON LAUE. I disagree. I think she's a quiet, caring sort of person. He is very protective of her.

HAHN. I very much doubt that Major Rittner's wife needs protecting.

VON LAUE. She's a blonde, with big blue eyes, and a wide-brimmed sunhat with a blue bow.

HAHN. Sounds like your Magda. I think she's dark, with black curls down to her elbows, and piercing green eyes.

VON LAUE. Sounds like Edith.

Pause.

Where do you think they met? Rittner and his wife.

HAHN. The war.

VON LAUE. This war?

HAHN. The last war.

VON LAUE. Major Rittner isn't a day over fifty. He was a child in the last war.

HAHN. He enlisted early and illegally. At fourteen.

VON LAUE. I think they met at the seaside.

HAHN. His elder brother had already been killed, so Rittner enlisted to avenge his death.

VON LAUE. Brighton. On a pier. At sunset.

HAHN. Rittner fought bravely, but he was wounded. The bullet skimmed his heart.

VON LAUE. She was standing at the end of the pier, watching the waves, when her hat was blown away by a particularly fortuitous gust of wind.

HAHN. He ended up in an army hospital. His future wife was a Red Cross nurse, slightly older than him. She tended to him.

VON LAUE. She tried to catch it, but it spiralled out of her reach, fell over the side of the pier, and landed in the water.

HAHN. She was intrigued. This man who was so young but so brave. He was taken with her, of course. She was so beautiful.

VON LAUE. Rittner witnessed all this and immediately dived into the sea to rescue the hat. He didn't even stop to remove his jacket.

HAHN. Just before he was to return to the Front, he declared his love for her.

VON LAUE. As he strode out of the waves, the hat clutched in his hand, she ran down the shore to meet him.

HAHN. She turned him down because of the war. It was all too uncertain.

VON LAUE. When they came together, she didn't even acknowledge the hat, she just threw her arms around him to keep him warm.

HAHN. But he survived the war, and they met again. At a train station. Victoria. The *Brighton* line. Many years later.

VON LAUE. He looked into her eyes, and he knew. He proposed, there and then.

HAHN. Their eyes met from distant ends of a platform.

VON LAUE. She said 'yes'.

HAHN. They knew it was more than a coincidence.

VON LAUE. It was fate.

They gaze into the distance, each preoccupied with their own romantic reverie.

VON LAUE *is the first to emerge from his daydream.*

I wonder which is closest to the truth. My blonde with the sunhat, or your dark-haired nurse.

HAHN. Perhaps his wife is German.

VON LAUE *looks at him.*

He speaks the language like a native!

VON LAUE. I think either version is equally unlikely. Mrs Rittner probably has brown hair, she's probably a kindergarten teacher, they probably met through friends. Real life is never so exciting.

Scene Six

The guests are gathered around the piano. WEIZSÄCKER *is playing Schubert's 'Die Forelle'. He finishes with a flourish and the guests applaud.*

WEIZSÄCKER. Stop, please. The applause should go to Von Laue and Hahn for their remarkable feat of carpentry. Pay attention, Diebner, Heisenberg. This is what happens when scientists collaborate rather than compete.

HEISENBERG. Weizsäcker, you're the most competitive person I know.

WEIZSÄCKER. No, I'm not.

BAGGE. I'm far more competitive than he is.

WEIZSÄCKER. You are not.

BAGGE. Heisenberg?

HEISENBERG. You're both equally competitive.

HAHN. Such an impartial parent.

WEIZSÄCKER. Right, what's next? 'Die Forelle'?

HAHN. Again?

WEIZSÄCKER. It's the only piece I know by heart.

HAHN. You play something, Heisenberg. Play your Bach.

WEIZSÄCKER. God forbid. None of Heisenberg's Bach, please. When we were in Haigerloch, he kept creeping off to a little baroque church to play the organ. It was very atmospheric, and extremely tedious. There we were, attempting to give birth to the Atomic Age, and Heisenberg was traipsing off to his lonely mountain to nurse his tortured soul. More Schubert!

WEIZSÄCKER *launches once more into 'Die Forelle'.*

I shall never grow tired of this piano!

Scene Seven

Later. The guests are silently writing letters – except DIEBNER, *who is reading a book, and* HEISENBERG, *who is absent.*

BAGGE. I don't think our letters are being sent.

HAHN. Why do you say that?

BAGGE. When was the last time any of us received a reply?

WEIZSÄCKER. Perhaps it's your wife who's not writing back, Bagge. Perhaps she's glad to be shot of you.

HAHN. Weizsäcker.

WEIZSÄCKER. How's this? 'Mama – I hope you are well, and not worrying too much about me. Console yourself with the knowledge that I am well and that the weather here is surprisingly very fine – '

DIEBNER. Redact.

WEIZSÄCKER. What?

DIEBNER. You'll have to redact that.

WEIZSÄCKER. Why?

DIEBNER. 'The weather here is surprisingly very fine.' Rittner's never going to let that through. Your mother could easily work out where you are.

WEIZSÄCKER. How?

DIEBNER. There's only one country in the world in which 'fine' weather is 'surprising'.

VON LAUE. I'm uncertain about mine now.

HAHN. Read it aloud, Von Laue.

VON LAUE. 'My darling Magda – it fills me with such indescribable relief to hear that you and the children are safe and well. We read in the *Daily Telegraph* – '

DIEBNER. Redact.

WEIZSÄCKER. You can get the *Telegraph* in other countries.

DIEBNER. He'll have to write the whole thing out again if he includes it.

Beat.

Also, no 'we'. You can't say 'we'.

VON LAUE. Why not?

BAGGE (*significantly*). Who's 'we'?

DIEBNER. Exactly.

BAGGE. They don't know we're together.

WEIZSÄCKER. They know.

DIEBNER. They don't, they assume. No 'we'.

VON LAUE. Very well.

He amends his letter.

'My darling Magda – it fills me with such indescribable relief to hear that you and the children are safe and well. I read somewhere – '

DIEBNER. Good.

VON LAUE. ' – that the Soviets have – '

DIEBNER. Redact.

VON LAUE. Why?

DIEBNER. No names. No places. No politics. No science.

WEIZSÄCKER. Major Rittner really is one for catchy slogans.

DIEBNER *closes his book and stands.*

Where are you going?

DIEBNER. I wasn't aware I was still needed.

WEIZSÄCKER. Of course you're needed, Diebner. You're always needed. Why don't you read your letter aloud?

DIEBNER. You know I'm not writing a letter.

WEIZSÄCKER. The self-proclaimed expert –

DIEBNER. – I never claimed to be an expert.

WEIZSÄCKER. – ought to show us how it's done.

DIEBNER. I'm not writing a letter.

WEIZSÄCKER. I know you're not married but you must have family or friends. *Someone* must care that you were spirited out of Germany in the middle of the night and haven't been seen since.

DIEBNER. No.

WEIZSÄCKER. Just pretend then. Show us how to evade Rittner's scrupulous censorship.

DIEBNER. Very well... 'Dear – '

WEIZSÄCKER. 'Führer!'

Beat.

DIEBNER. Hysterical. 'Dear Führer – I do hope the war is going well.'

WEIZSÄCKER. Do it properly, Diebner. No names, no places, no politics, no science.

DIEBNER. 'Dear Führer – for breakfast I had non-descript cereal.'

WEIZSÄCKER. Good.

DIEBNER. 'When I woke up it was neither light nor dark, nor hot nor cold.'

WEIZSÄCKER. Excellent.

DIEBNER. 'Today, I might read a book, but then again, maybe not.'

WEIZSÄCKER. Exactly! Throw them off the scent.

DIEBNER. 'Weizsäcker made me – '

BAGGE. Redact! No names, no places, no politics, no science!

DIEBNER (*tiredly*). Hurrah!

WEIZSÄCKER *claps*.

BAGGE. Not that it matters. Our self-censorship. Not if I'm right and our letters aren't being sent.

HAHN. That is rather distrusting of you, Bagge. I shouldn't like to think so poorly of our hosts.

BAGGE. I shouldn't like to think a lot of things, Hahn, but we must reconcile ourselves to the fact that we will be assassinated in our beds before too long and no one will ever know what happened to us.

WEIZSÄCKER. Isn't there some code against executing POWs?

HAHN. We're civilian scientists, Weizsäcker, not soldiers.

DIEBNER. Is there a difference?

HAHN. Stop worrying. We'll be home with our families before that letter reaches them, anyway.

WEIZSÄCKER. Will we?

VON LAUE. Will we?

HAHN. I, for one, think we'll be allowed to go home very soon.

VON LAUE. How soon?

HAHN. Soon-ish.

BAGGE. 'Ish.'

VON LAUE. How soon-ish?

HAHN. Imminently.

BAGGE. Imminently-ish.

HAHN. By Christmas, I think, at the latest.

WEIZSÄCKER. I must say, I disagree.

DIEBNER. Must you?

WEIZSÄCKER. You're being far too optimistic, Hahn. I think the probability of our being home by Christmas very slim.

VON LAUE. How slim?

WEIZSÄCKER. Five per cent. Perhaps ten.

HAHN. But the possibility of our never getting home at all –

WEIZSÄCKER. Oh, seventy or seventy-five per cent. I consider it likely.

Pause.

HAHN. Perhaps we should write to one of our friends here in England.

VON LAUE. Do we have any friends left in England?

HAHN. Patrick Blackett? He's in Cambridge.

DIEBNER. Manchester.

HAHN. Still, perhaps we could ask him to speak to someone on our behalf.

VON LAUE. I'm not sure if a letter from any of us would be particularly well-received.

DIEBNER. Rittner won't let you write to Blackett, anyway. They don't want it out that we're here.

BAGGE. What do they want? What do they want with us?

WEIZSÄCKER. These English Heydrichs and Kaltenbrunners.

DIEBNER. I don't think they know.

WEIZSÄCKER. That's the awful thing about the English. It takes them ages to make up their minds.

DIEBNER. The Empire has been built over centuries. They can't understand it when someone is in a rush.

WEIZSÄCKER *laughs.* HEISENBERG *enters with the newspaper.*

HEISENBERG. Do we care about cricket?

ALL. No.

HEISENBERG. Someone has given evidence in someone else's trial.

WEIZSÄCKER. How many letters?

HEISENBERG. The first someone... five. The second... six. The trial itself has been deemed 'unreasonable'.

DIEBNER. The six might be Pétain.

WEIZSÄCKER. Or Stalin? Truman? Or Attlee!

HAHN. Pétain, surely.

HEISENBERG. It's Pétain.

WEIZSÄCKER. And the five?

HEISENBERG. Laval. A treaty has been signed somewhere.

WEIZSÄCKER. How many letters?

HEISENBERG. Seven.

WEIZSÄCKER. A city?

HEISENBERG. Yes.

WEIZSÄCKER. In Germany?

HEISENBERG. Yes.

WEIZSÄCKER. Hamburg?

HAHN. Cologne?

BAGGE. Leipzig?

DIEBNER. Dresden?

HEISENBERG. Potsdam. And Thuringia is now occupied by the Soviets.

Silence.

WEIZSÄCKER. Bagge, isn't your wife...?

BAGGE. Yes, in Stadtilm. Can I see?

He takes the paper from HEISENBERG. *Silence.*

What should I do?

HAHN. Talk to Rittner. He might be able to help.

BAGGE. What can he do?

HAHN. Perhaps he can move her.

BAGGE. Why would he? Why would he help me?

HAHN. He's a good man. If he can help, I'm certain he will.

BAGGE. Rittner doesn't like me, I know he doesn't.

Beat.

(*Crying.*) She's completely alone.

WEIZSÄCKER. Don't get upset. She'll be all right.

He tries to put his arm around BAGGE*'s shoulders.*

BAGGE. Get off me! You don't know. Your family's in
Switzerland. You don't have anything to worry about.
Heisenberg's wife is in the American zone, so is yours –
(*To* HAHN.) and yours – (*To* VON LAUE.) None of you
know what it is like to, to –

He runs out of the room.

Scene Eight

Later. All the guests except HAHN. *Very frustrated and
bored now.*

BAGGE (*quietly*). When will we go home?

HEISENBERG. Soon.

BAGGE. I don't know how much longer I can bear it.

WEIZSÄCKER. He's right. Why are we still here? If it's to do
with our work on uranium, then, no offence meant, but why
is Von Laue here? You weren't involved at all in our
research. Same goes for Hahn. Where is Hahn?

HEISENBERG. With Rittner.

VON LAUE. Perhaps we are being punished, not protected.

WEIZSÄCKER. If we're being punished, then where are
Lenard and Stark?

BAGGE. Exactly.

WEIZSÄCKER. I think it rather unfair that we should be
persecuted while Hitler's greatest scientific allies are

evidently walking around, at home, in Germany, without
a care in the world –

DIEBNER. Lenard and Stark are probably dead, Weizsäcker.

WEIZSÄCKER. I mean so one would hope, but we've no
guarantee that's the case.

Beat.

And punished for what, Von Laue? What did I do? What did
you do? As for Heisenberg, Lenard and Stark called him
a 'White Jew' when he refused to stop teaching relativity.
They almost got him sacked. 'The spirit of Einstein's spirit' –
they wrote that in the paper. Why would we be punished
when we behaved well?

VON LAUE. Not all of us behaved well.

Silence.

DIEBNER. Here it is.

BAGGE (*agitated*). Von Laue, I think I should –

HEISENBERG. Bagge, he didn't mean –

BAGGE. He did. He meant it and I'm sick to death of it.
(*To* VON LAUE.) If you have something to say, then say it.

VON LAUE. Fine. You are a Nazi, and so is Diebner.

HEISENBERG. That's enough.

VON LAUE. Why do you defend them?

HEISENBERG. The fact of being a Party member doesn't
necessarily tell against a man.

VON LAUE. Yes, it does.

BAGGE. But it wasn't my choice!

VON LAUE *scoffs.*

It was my mother, she thought it was a good idea. She sent
my name in and I didn't know anything about it. And a few
months later I got my Party book, and it said that I had sworn
an oath to Hitler, which I didn't do.

VON LAUE. You were in the SA.

BAGGE. We all were! All the assistants. Wirtz, Bopp, Renner, Welker. It was compulsory.

VON LAUE. I didn't join the Teachers' Union. They sent letters and made threats. I just threw everything in the bin.

DIEBNER (*quietly*). That's one way of doing it.

BAGGE. But you must understand –

VON LAUE. No, it's not right to say that you *had* to do anything –

BAGGE. We're not the same –

HEISENBERG (*to* VON LAUE). I will say that you and Bagge were at different stages of your career. You had a reputation that went some way to protect you, Von Laue, you know that. Bagge did not.

BAGGE. Do you remember Euler? Another of Heisenberg's assistants? He didn't get a job in Leipzig because he wasn't a Party member. The fight lasted eighteen months and not even Heisenberg could manage it. I needed to work, and –

HEISENBERG. His family's poor. He did what was expected of him. The same expectations can't apply.

VON LAUE. Because he is poor?

BAGGE. My father is a locksmith.

HEISENBERG. Yes.

BAGGE. And when I heard about anything bad – and I never heard much about, you know, the camps, and things like that – but when I did, I always condemned it. Strongly.

VON LAUE. And that is all you can say for yourself?

BAGGE (*breaking down*). I wanted to do well. Is that so wrong? I just wanted to do well.

Silence.

VON LAUE. And you, Diebner?

DIEBNER. Hm?

VON LAUE. What do you say for yourself.

DIEBNER. Ah, everyone knows my views.

VON LAUE. You're a Party man.

DIEBNER. And yet I did so much to help people. I stopped the institute in Copenhagen from being touched. I prevented the removal of their cyclotron. I stopped our colleagues from being arrested in Norway. I tried to get Pienkowski out of Poland. I helped Joliot with the Gestapo. Does that count for nothing?

VON LAUE. Remind me, what happened to Pienkowski?

DIEBNER. That was the Russians. The point is, I tried. And while we're pointing fingers, none of us are unimpeachable. I joined the Party to protect and progress my career.

(*To* WEIZSÄCKER.) We can't all rely on a father in the Foreign Office.

(*To* HEISENBERG.) Or a family friend in Heinrich Himmler.

Pause.

Isn't that right, Heisenberg? As I recall, you stayed in post because your mother wrote a letter and then Frau Himmler wrote a letter and then Himmler himself wrote two letters. One to Heydrich and one to yourself. Letters of recommendation.

HEISENBERG. That's not the same.

DIEBNER. It *is* the same. The fact is, just as Von Laue was protected by his reputation, you were protected by your connections. Connections you were more than willing to exploit.

HEISENBERG. My mother knew Himmler, yes, but that is not the same as gleefully engaging in Party politics. Grabbing at every available scrap of power to advance your own career.

DIEBNER. I am not ashamed of what I've done. I did what was best for myself and what I thought was best for Germany.

HEISENBERG *scoffs.*

I did as much as I could when I could. You deign to judge
me –

HEISENBERG. I do judge you.

DIEBNER. And Bagge?

BAGGE *shakes his head.*

HEISENBERG. And what you thought was 'best for Germany'.

DIEBNER. But who applied for Max Born's professorship
when he was suspended? Who didn't lift a finger to stop it?
You were grabbing at power just as I was, but instead of
admitting it, you conceal, and hide, and rewrite history –

HAHN *enters. He is visibly disturbed.*

– to cast yourself in the best possible light.

HEISENBERG. Hahn.

VON LAUE. Are you all right?

HAHN. Yes. I must, I must tell you something.

HEISENBERG. You're unwell.

HAHN. No, I –

VON LAUE (*gently*). What is it?

HAHN. I might as well come out and say it. The Americans
have built an atom bomb. They have dropped it on Japan.

End of Act One.

ACT TWO

Scene Nine

We follow straight on from the end of Act One, Scene Eight.

WEIZSÄCKER. What?

DIEBNER. Say that again, Hahn.

HAHN. The Americans have built an atom bomb, and they have used it against Japan.

Pause.

VON LAUE. Oh my God...

BAGGE. When?

HAHN. This morning.

Pause.

WEIZSÄCKER. But that isn't –

VON LAUE. Hahn –

BAGGE. How?

WEIZSÄCKER. Who told you?

HAHN. Rittner, just now.

WEIZSÄCKER. Who told him?

HAHN. His government, I assume.

VON LAUE. Has Japan surrendered?

WEIZSÄCKER. Go and get him. I want to hear it from him.

BAGGE. How?

HAHN. I don't know.

WEIZSÄCKER. I'll get him. Hahn, where's Rittner?

HAHN. He's gone.

WEIZSÄCKER. What? Where?

HAHN. London, I think. He didn't say.

WEIZSÄCKER. But what about us?

HAHN. What about us?

Silence.

Rittner has given us a radio. (*He places it on the table.*)
There will be a broadcast at nine o'clock. He thought we
might like to hear it.

Pause.

BAGGE (*tentatively, to* HEISENBERG *more than anyone else*).
How have they done it? I thought... at least not so soon.

Silence.

WEIZSÄCKER. Heisenberg?

HEISENBERG. It's not an atom bomb.

HAHN. What?

HEISENBERG. It can't be. It's something else.

BAGGE. Why would Rittner lie?

HEISENBERG. I don't think he's lying, just misinformed.

HAHN. Heisenberg.

HEISENBERG. Did Rittner mention 'uranium'?

Beat.

HAHN. No.

HEISENBERG. There we are, then.

HAHN. But he wouldn't've known the word, Heisenberg. He's
not a scientist.

HEISENBERG. Clearly.

Pause.

WEIZSÄCKER. If they have made a bomb, they were damn
good at keeping it a secret.

HEISENBERG. 'If.'

WEIZSÄCKER. I said 'if'.

DIEBNER. Goudsmit lied to our faces. He spent days questioning us. He made it seem like the Allies weren't even close, that they hadn't even tried. What a laugh he must have had at our expense.

BAGGE. They were watching us the whole time.

DIEBNER. We were watching them. And we still couldn't get it.

HAHN. Yes, it does make one feel rather second-rate. Poor old Heisenberg.

Beat.

That was a joke.

DIEBNER. I wouldn't joke if I were you. Heisenberg's very upset. He's just found out there are people who can do something he can't. Americans, no less.

HEISENBERG. Why are you all so eager to accept this?

HAHN. 'Eager'?

HEISENBERG. It's just a bluff to get us to reveal how far we'd got.

DIEBNER. You're deluded.

HEISENBERG. What proof do we have that this is real? Other than the frankly tenuous word of Major Rittner? It's just cruelty on their part.

Beat.

VON LAUE. Oh, dear.

DIEBNER. I never thought you were so enamoured with your own genius that –

HEISENBERG. Not my genius, Diebner. Germany's genius. Please think for a moment. Does this make sense? Does it make sense that American science…? What is American science, anyway? She is a nation of no originality. A thief of men, a poor appropriator of ideas. Ford robbed Benz of the automobile! Anderson robbed Hess of the glory of cosmic rays! Priestley robbed Scheele of oxygen!

BAGGE (*quietly*). Priestley was English...

HEISENBERG. And here, again, America has hijacked another German discovery – Hahn's nuclear fission – to play some cheap trick!

Beat.

WEIZSÄCKER (*calmly*). Do you remember when we first met, Heisenberg?

HEISENBERG. What? Yes.

WEIZSÄCKER. No, you don't. I know you don't. Not the first time.

I was fourteen. We bumped into each other at a railway station in Berlin and caught a taxi together. My mother already knew you, through Bohr, I suppose, and she introduced us. We had a long talk and I remember feeling struck that here, finally, was a person who knew everything better than I did. Physics, mathematics, languages, music. I distinctly remember you talking about having refuted the laws of causality. It was during that taxi ride with you that I became determined to study physics, so that one day I could understand exactly what you'd meant.

When we started, I was convinced that if you couldn't do it, it couldn't be done.

HEISENBERG. It can't be done.

WEIZSÄCKER. It can because they have done it.

Scene Ten

Almost nine o'clock. Each of the guests is clasping a glass of gin.

A radio sits on a table, quietly playing music.

DIEBNER *checks his watch.*

DIEBNER. Eight fifty-seven.

BAGGE (*holding the bottle of gin*). More?

HAHN. Yes, please.

BAGGE. Heisenberg?

> HEISENBERG *shakes his head.*

DIEBNER. Here.

> BAGGE *tops up his drink. He holds the bottle up to*
> WEIZSÄCKER, *who shakes his head.* BAGGE *shuffles*
> *awkwardly around* VON LAUE.

BAGGE (*tentatively*). Professor Von Laue?

VON LAUE. Thank you.

> BAGGE *refills* VON LAUE's *glass, and then his own.*
> *The bottle is empty.*

BAGGE. That was quick.

HAHN. There's more in the kitchen.

BAGGE. I'll get it.

DIEBNER. Eight fifty-eight.

BAGGE. I'll wait.

> *A long silence.*

> VON LAUE *squeezes* HAHN's *knee.*

> WEIZSÄCKER *tries to catch* HEISENBERG's *eye.*

> BAGGE *floats around the room.*

> DIEBNER *sips his gin, counting down the time in his head.*

DIEBNER. Eight fifty-nine.

BAGGE. It's like waiting for an exam result.

HAHN. Turn it up, Weizsäcker, will you?

WEIZSÄCKER. I will when the time comes.

DIEBNER. Thirty seconds. Twenty-five, twenty-four, twenty-three, twenty-two –

RADIO (*voice-over*). This is the BBC –

HAHN. Turn it up.

WEIZSÄCKER *does*.

RADIO. Here is the news. It's dominated by a tremendous achievement of Allied scientists – the production of an atomic bomb. One has already been dropped on the Japanese war base of Hiroshima. It alone contained as much explosive power as two thousand of the RAF's ten-tonne bombs of orthodox design. President Truman has told how the bombs were produced in secret American factories. Up to a hundred and twenty-five thousand people helped to build the factories, and at present, sixty-five thousand people are operating them. The Allies have spent five hundred million pounds on what President Truman calls the greatest scientific gamble in history – and they've won. British, American, and Canadian scientists have succeeded, where the Germans failed, in harnessing the basic power of the universe.

There's no news yet of what devastation was caused after the bomb had landed. Airmen reported that the city of once over three hundred thousand inhabitants, was completely hidden by an impenetrable cloud of smoke and dust.

At home, it's been a bank holiday of sunshine and showers...

WEIZSÄCKER *switches off the radio*.

DIEBNER. Satisfied, Heisenberg?

Pause.

How have they done it?

HAHN. I suggest we –

DIEBNER. Well?

HAHN. What's the use, Diebner, of dwelling –

DIEBNER. The use, Hahn, is that I find it a disgrace if we, the physicists who worked on it, you, the man who made it possible in the first place, cannot understand how an atom bomb has been produced, in theory, at the very least?

BAGGE. He said 'bombs'. More than one. How can that be?

WEIZSÄCKER. Heisenberg?

HEISENBERG. You heard him. Secret factories, hundreds of thousands of people. Five hundred million pounds. 'The greatest scientific gamble in history.'

BAGGE. But how have they manufactured enough uranium-two-three-five? That's nothing to do with secret factories or money or men, that's technique. You always said we would need two tonnes of U-two-three-five to do anything.

HAHN. Two tonnes?

BAGGE. How could they have manufactured enough U-two-three-five for more than one bomb?

HEISENBERG. They must have a method of separating isotopes of which we have no idea.

HAHN. I thought you needed very little U-two-three-five?

WEIZSÄCKER. Diffusion separation?

DIEBNER. That's what I was doing.

WEIZSÄCKER. Yes, but we only had one man working on it. They had thousands.

HAHN. Heisenberg?

HEISENBERG. Hm?

HAHN. I thought you needed very little uranium-two-three-five for a bomb? You told me it would take fifty kilograms, now Bagge says two tonnes.

DIEBNER. Fifty kilograms?

HEISENBERG. I wouldn't like to commit myself to any figure right now.

DIEBNER. But which is it? Fifty kilograms or two tonnes?

HEISENBERG. Does it matter?

DIEBNER. Of course it does.

WEIZSÄCKER. Settle down, Diebner.

DIEBNER (*to* WEIZSÄCKER). What did he tell you? Fifty kilograms or two tonnes?

Beat.

WEIZSÄCKER. I don't remember.

DIEBNER. You don't remember?

HEISENBERG. Diebner –

DIEBNER. In 1942, I wrote a report to the Army Weapons Agency. I asked for permission to move from theoretical research to full-scale development. I said that it would take ten to one hundred kilograms of U-two-three-five to build a bomb, but I was overruled by *you*, by *your* group, and by *your* estimate of critical mass which was at least twenty times greater than mine.

BAGGE. Perhaps they've done it some other way –

DIEBNER. Twenty times more uranium! Twenty times more difficult! Twenty times more expensive! Twenty times more unobtainable!

BAGGE. Perhaps they've done it with protactinium.

DIEBNER. Is it any wonder we didn't get anywhere?

BAGGE. Or element ninety-four.

DIEBNER. Is it any wonder when you were undermining me at every available turn? When you were pulling numbers out of thin air and turning the authorities against us, diverting our funds towards, what, rockets?

HEISENBERG. Diebner –

DIEBNER. Von Braun's rockets?

Which is it, Heisenberg? Fifty kilograms or two tonnes?

Silence.

Eventually, HAHN *snorts and starts to laugh. The others look at him.*

WEIZSÄCKER. Have you gone mad?

HAHN (*still laughing*). No, no. I'm just happy.

They continue to stare.

Bagge, aren't you thrilled that the Americans have done it?

BAGGE. I –

WEIZSÄCKER. Why should he be thrilled?

HAHN. Can you imagine if we had been the first to use such a weapon?

BAGGE. I was afraid of the bomb, of course, but I did think it was right that we, I mean Germany, should be the first ones to make use of a German discovery. Don't you think, Heisenberg?

HEISENBERG. It would have been a much greater tragedy if we had got there first.

BAGGE. But what were we working for?

WEIZSÄCKER. If we *had* got there first, Diebner would be sitting in Luxembourg as a war criminal.

DIEBNER. You'd be sitting next to me.

WEIZSÄCKER. That's only if we'd lost, I suppose. Perhaps with the bomb we might have conquered the world.

DIEBNER. We might have obliterated London, but we still wouldn't have conquered the world.

WEIZSÄCKER. London, you think? Not an American city?

DIEBNER. What do you mean?

WEIZSÄCKER. I mean, is that where we would have chosen? If we'd got the bomb first?

BAGGE. Washington, surely. Or New York.

WEIZSÄCKER. Not Washington.

BAGGE. Why not?

WEIZSÄCKER. We wouldn't have wanted to totally eradicate the American leadership. Who would negotiate the surrender?

BAGGE. San Diego? Headquarters of the American Navy.

DIEBNER. How exactly are you planning on delivering an atom bomb to the west coast of the United States?

BAGGE. In an aeroplane.

DIEBNER. You'd pitch into the Atlantic.

WEIZSÄCKER. Europe, then. London.

DIEBNER. At least that's somewhat realistic.

WEIZSÄCKER. Coventry, perhaps. Southampton.

BAGGE. What about Russia? Stalingrad? If we'd got it early enough, who knows what might have happened?

WEIZSÄCKER. That would have been something.

DIEBNER. We never would have got it that early.

WEIZSÄCKER. We're just imagining, Diebner. It's only a game.

Pause.

What happens when an atom bomb explodes?

Can you picture it?

Pause. WEIZSÄCKER *goes to the window.*

It will have been lighter when it happened, of course. Early morning, clear and bright.

BAGGE. So the pilot can see the target?

WEIZSÄCKER. Yes, but also because bad weather might absorb the thermal radiation and limit the damage caused by fire. They will have chosen a clear day.

A single bomb is dropped at a height of, oh, ten thousand metres. Our man in the aircraft makes a hasty getaway. The bomb careers down to earth and, a few hundred metres from the ground, explodes –

BAGGE. How?

WEIZSÄCKER. Somehow.

If we make the centre of the explosion that field across the road, opposite the front of the house. Anything within a mile of that field would be vaporised, in an instant. Temperatures exceeding ten million degrees Celsius.

DIEBNER. Including us, of course. The Hall, the house at the end of the garden, and everyone inside of it.

BAGGE. Including Rittner.

WEIZSÄCKER. We wouldn't live long enough see the light. And the noise – the rumble of energy – would come seconds after we were gone.

Beat.

Say that we survived, say each of us was encased in an indestructible suit of lead or gold... What would we see? On the other side of the road?

DIEBNER. Nothing. A blizzard of earth and smoke. A sky on fire.

WEIZSÄCKER. And if we were in a city, a large city. What then? What would happen to the people?

DIEBNER. Those who weren't killed instantly by the blast –

BAGGE. Or crushed by the rubble.

WEIZSÄCKER. What would happen to them?

DIEBNER. Who knows? Dirty poison loosed a mile wide. Collecting in our lungs, in the river...

Beat. HAHN *shifts uncomfortably in his seat.*

Those women... do you remember? The workers who painted watch dials with radium so you could tell the time in the dark. They swallowed lethal amounts of radium paint by wetting the paintbrushes with their lips. Their mouths began to rot. Teeth fell out. Bleeding gums refused to heal. Their skin split –

HAHN *walks out.*

HEISENBERG. Hahn –

VON LAUE (*disgusted*). You're enjoying this. You're relishing it.

WEIZSÄCKER. Do not mistake objectivity for relish, Von Laue.

VON LAUE. Hahn is your friend, Heisenberg. How can you sit there and let him be tormented like that? Though you are evidently incapable of shame, you can surely recognise it in others.

WEIZSÄCKER. What does Hahn have to be ashamed of?

VON LAUE. Are you dense?

WEIZSÄCKER. No, Von Laue. I just don't understand why Hahn should feel ashamed. Responsibility, perhaps –

VON LAUE. They're the same. His responsibility and his shame go hand in hand.

WEIZSÄCKER. They don't have to. You can feel responsible without feeling ashamed. Hahn discovered nuclear fission; the Americans have used fission to build a bomb. Ergo and not illogically, Hahn feels responsible. But what does he have to be ashamed of?

HEISENBERG. Von Laue –

VON LAUE. No more, Heisenberg. I don't want to hear it. You're answerable to someone, but not to me.

He is in the doorway when he turns back.

If we don't die, I think we will now, but if we don't, many questions will be asked of us. I know what I will say.

Scene Eleven

HAHN *and* VON LAUE.

VON LAUE. Can I get you something? A glass of water?

HAHN. No, thank you.

VON LAUE. I don't know what to say.

HAHN. I'm all right.

VON LAUE. I'm so ashamed of the others.

HAHN. Don't be.

VON LAUE. I'm so angry.

HAHN. Don't be.

VON LAUE. It doesn't do me any good.

HAHN. They're excited. It's exciting.

VON LAUE. Don't excuse them.

HAHN. Why not? What does it matter?

   Pause.

VON LAUE. It isn't your fault. You're not to blame.

HAHN. I am to blame.

   Beat.

   Three hundred thousand people, Max. How am I to bear it?

   Pause.

   I can't bear it. I won't.

VON LAUE. Don't say that. Don't ever – how can you hold yourself responsible, Otto? It was the Americans who built the thing and pressed the button.

   Pause.

   Do you remember my assistant, Szilard?

HAHN. He liked long baths.

VON LAUE. Before he went to America, he told me a story.
It was back in 1933 and he was in London. He'd just
attended a lecture by Rutherford, and he stopped at a set of
traffic lights opposite the British Museum. As the traffic
lights changed colour, Szilard saw the end of the world. He
imagined an uncontrollable chain reaction, an explosion
mightier than anything in history. It paralysed him. And then
the light turned from green to amber and red, and Szilard
was back again. No chain reaction, no explosion. But he had
seen it. That was 1933.

Do you understand what I'm trying to say? We all knew
what it meant, Hahn. For all Rutherford's talk of
'moonshine', we all thought it was a possibility. It's the
nature of scientific discovery. If it hadn't been you, it would
have been someone else.

Scene Twelve

The others.

WEIZSÄCKER. It's terrible for Hahn, of course. He really did
do it.

Pause.

DIEBNER. He's right.

WEIZSÄCKER. Who?

DIEBNER. Von Laue. What will we say?

BAGGE. When? To who?

DIEBNER. Everyone. To the Allies. To Germany.

BAGGE. When?

DIEBNER. When we are released.

WEIZSÄCKER. *If* we are released.

DIEBNER. If we are released, what will we tell them?

HEISENBERG. The truth.

DIEBNER. And what's that?

BAGGE. I don't understand.

DIEBNER. What is the truth?

WEIZSÄCKER. That we can't tell them anything. We don't
know anything.

DIEBNER. Exactly. We thought we had some special
knowledge to barter with, but we don't.

WEIZSÄCKER. So?

DIEBNER. So, when Hitler came to power the most righteous
course of action would have been to follow Von Laue or
Hahn's precedent. To have spoken out, to have condemned,
to have resigned our posts in protest. But we didn't do that.
We didn't do that and, as a result, each of us is here. We are
here and we need something to say.

They look at him.

We need something to tell them, and it can't be that we
didn't do anything. It can't be that we didn't know anything.
We tried to build an atom bomb for –

BAGGE (*quickly*). No, we didn't.

DIEBNER. Oh, Bagge, we did.

BAGGE. No, listen to me, Diebner. Perhaps *you* did, but we
didn't. We weren't trying to build the bomb *for him*. It
wasn't ever about him, or the Reich, or the war. It wasn't
even about Germany. It was about physics. It was about
using Hahn's discovery to –

DIEBNER. You want to pretend that we were just idly doing
our work, with no idea what might be done with it. Bagge,
he paid for our research. And if we had succeeded, he would
have taken what he paid for, and he would have used it.

BAGGE. But –

DIEBNER. No, Bagge. No 'but'. Are you suggesting that we might have kept an atom bomb secret from Hitler? That we could have taken the money, our commission, and run?

BAGGE. Maybe –

DIEBNER *groans*.

Heisenberg said that we were channelling all the chaos towards something productive. That we were putting the war in the service of science, not the other way around.

HEISENBERG (*quietly*). The world is ugly, but the work is beautiful.

DIEBNER. A pretty maxim, but entirely irrelevant. Who cares what our agenda was? If we were being used, or doing the using? If we had succeeded, the result would always have been the same. We knew that. The Allies know that we knew that.

WEIZSÄCKER. We didn't succeed, so why does it matter?

DIEBNER. It's a moral question, Weizsäcker. What sort of person would even try?

WEIZSÄCKER. The Americans tried. They tried, they succeeded. We aren't any worse than them.

DIEBNER. Hitler was a criminal.

WEIZSÄCKER. You joined his Party!

DIEBNER. Yes, and I will have to explain that as well.

Silence.

BAGGE (*tentatively*). But we never... really *tried*... did we? In every discussion we had – with Speer in '42, for example – we always concluded that it was difficult, expensive, that it would take a long time. That it wasn't a weapon for this war, but the next. We tried to build a bomb, yes, but with a great deal of restraint.

WEIZSÄCKER. Hence Heisenberg's two tonnes.

DIEBNER (*to* HEISENBERG). How convenient for you. Was that your plan all along then? You were trying to put them off? Heisenberg?

BAGGE. Can't we tell them that? They'd like that, wouldn't they? That we tried to, you know, dampen enthusiasm for the project? We have evidence: Heisenberg's incorrect estimates. Weizsäcker and I destroyed our work, but in reports, in the minutes of meetings… It's all there.

Pause.

HEISENBERG. No.

WEIZSÄCKER. No?

HEISENBERG. We can't say that.

BAGGE. Why not?

HEISENBERG. That might placate the British and the Americans, but it will turn our countrymen against us. You want to tell Germany that I, *we*, purposefully sabotaged –

BAGGE. Slowed.

HEISENBERG. Slowed, sabotaged, whatever. You want to say that we purposefully didn't build a bomb that might have won us the war.

WEIZSÄCKER. No one wanted Hitler to win by the end.

HEISENBERG. No one wanted Germany to lose either. You're too young to remember what it was like after the last war –

WEIZSÄCKER. I'm thirty-three.

HEISENBERG. Then you're too privileged.

DIEBNER. I remember.

HEISENBERG. If we tell Germany that we staged a passive resistance, that we chose not to build a weapon that might have won us the war, we will be held responsible for whatever comes next. The consequences of our defeat, whatever they might be, will be our fault.

BAGGE. We'll be shot in the street.

Silence.

So, what do we say? If we can't say we chose not to do it –

DIEBNER. We say we couldn't do it.

Beat.

WEIZSÄCKER. I don't like it.

DIEBNER. Neither do I. But it's the truth, isn't it?

WEIZSÄCKER. No one will believe it, Diebner. It's preposterous.

They all wanted him. The British and the Americans. They all wanted Heisenberg to come and work for them. They won't believe that he, of all people, couldn't do it.

DIEBNER. But Heisenberg couldn't do it. Heisenberg didn't do it.

WEIZSÄCKER. We'll have to think of something else.

DIEBNER. Heisenberg can't do everything.

BAGGE. I'm beginning to come around to that way of thinking.

DIEBNER. Blasphemy, Bagge, you faithless disciple.

Pause.

What is the truth, Heisenberg? Now is the time to tell us. What happened? Could you do it?

Pause.

HEISENBERG. Circumstances being what they were –

DIEBNER. No, no, no. That's not the question. Could you do it?

WEIZSÄCKER. Yes.

DIEBNER. Weizsäcker.

WEIZSÄCKER. Yes, he could. He can.

BAGGE. Then why didn't he?

DIEBNER (*to* WEIZSÄCKER). I'm not asking you.

HEISENBERG. Circumstances being what they were, I couldn't do it.

DIEBNER. Then that is what we'll tell them.

WEIZSÄCKER. Jealousy is such an ugly trait, Diebner.

HEISENBERG (*to* DIEBNER). Aren't you going to ask why?

DIEBNER. Why what?

HEISENBERG. Why I couldn't do it? What circumstances specifically prevented me from doing it?

DIEBNER. Isn't it obvious? You weren't clever enough. Neither was I. I readily admit it.

HEISENBERG. A lack of trust. The trust wasn't there.

DIEBNER. Between you and me? Damn right it wasn't.

HEISENBERG. No, not between you and me. Between the scientists and the regime. They didn't trust us enough.

DIEBNER. They trusted us.

HEISENBERG. No, they may have trusted you and your group.

DIEBNER. Evidently not enough to accept my estimate of ten to one hundred kilograms.

HEISENBERG. That was their folly. They didn't trust my group –

DIEBNER. Academics in your ivory tower.

HEISENBERG. They trusted you and your military men, but not enough.

Beat.

The fact that Hitler encouraged rivalry between our groups didn't help much either. Is it any wonder we didn't succeed when we were encouraged to undermine each other all the time?

DIEBNER. Your inflated and contrary estimates of critical mass.

HEISENBERG. Your absconding with our uranium and heavy water.

WEIZSÄCKER. We chased you across Germany.

DIEBNER. You should have shared.

HEISENBERG. Perhaps if you had asked nicely.

The trust wasn't there. The resources weren't there.

DIEBNER. We had to fight for the resources that we did have.

HEISENBERG. And if we had asked for more, more money, more resources, and had failed?

DIEBNER. We would have had our heads cut off.

HEISENBERG. The truth is we were spared any moral decision because there isn't a world in which we could have succeeded. Confronted by a distrusting government, a thrifty government, a violent and unpredictable government –

WEIZSÄCKER. A government that had already scared away the brightest and best of our colleagues. Present company excluded. Who knows what might have happened if our Jewish colleagues had been allowed to stay?

Beat.

DIEBNER. Yes.

WEIZSÄCKER. Albert Einstein. Hans Bethe.

BAGGE. Lise Meitner. John von Neumann.

DIEBNER. Edward Teller. Fermi. Ulam.

WEIZSÄCKER. Franck and Wigner.

HEISENBERG. Max Born.

WEIZSÄCKER. What might have happened had they still been in the picture?

HEISENBERG. Circumstances being as they were –

BAGGE. But other areas flourished. Von Braun succeeded without the Jews.

WEIZSÄCKER. The Führer did always have a penchant for rockets, though, didn't he?

DIEBNER. And no real understanding of what *we* were trying to do, anyway.

BAGGE. Didn't he ask if an atom bomb would be powerful enough to throw a man from his horse?

HEISENBERG. A distrusting government, a thrifty government, a violent government, an ignorant government, a government with a penchant for rockets above everything else. We were spared any moral decision because we never stood a chance. It's a miracle we got as far as we did.

WEIZSÄCKER. With our uranium engine.

Beat.

Not a bomb. Never a bomb. The bomb was immaterial. The real coup would have been, and always was, a functioning uranium engine to –

BAGGE. To produce elements –

DIEBNER. To calculate the weight of atoms –

WEIZSÄCKER. To provide a substitute for fuel.

BAGGE. Yes.

WEIZSÄCKER. An engine of untold possibility. For the good of mankind.

Beat.

History will remember that. It will remember that, while America produced a heinous weapon of war, it was us, it was Germany who strove for a peaceful creation… Our uranium engine.

Scene Thirteen

Early morning. HEISENBERG *is surrounded by papers.*
HAHN *appears in the doorway.*

HAHN. Heisenberg?

HEISENBERG. Hahn.

HAHN. What're you doing?

HEISENBERG. I couldn't sleep.

HAHN. I don't think anyone can. Diebner and Bagge have been
   in and out of each other's rooms all night. Von Laue came in
   to see me twice. First, to borrow some soap. The second time
   more surreptitiously. A fluffy white head poked around the
   door. I think he was checking up on me.

HEISENBERG. He's worried you're going to kill yourself.

   HAHN *chuckles.*

   Are you?

HAHN. Going to kill myself?

   HAHN *thinks.*

   Not before I see Edith.

HEISENBERG. You know you aren't to blame for any of it.

HAHN. I've already had all this from Von Laue.

HEISENBERG. He's right.

   Pause. HAHN *scrutinises* HEISENBERG.

HAHN. You haven't been in to see me.

HEISENBERG. I needed time.

HAHN. To nurse your tortured soul, as Weizsäcker so delicately
   puts it.

   Beat.

   Are you tortured?

HEISENBERG. A little. I want to go home. And I'm afraid.

   Pause.

HAHN. Hm.

HEISENBERG. What?

HAHN. You're so impenetrable to me, Heisenberg. You're the only one whose secret thoughts I cannot read.

Beat.

What are you afraid of?

HEISENBERG. I'm not sure I know.

HAHN. Are you afraid you'll be killed?

HEISENBERG. No.

HAHN. That you'll be put in prison?

HEISENBERG. No.

Pause.

It won't ever be the same.

HAHN. No, but that's all right.

Silence. HAHN *gazes out of the window.*

Ah, the changing of the guard. We've not been totally abandoned then. A bleary-eyed boy. Do you think he has any idea what he's guarding?

Right. I shall take his arrival as my cue. It's far too early. What a miserable, miserable morning.

HAHN *begins to leave, but notices* HEISENBERG*'s papers.*

What's this?

HEISENBERG. Oh, an atom bomb.

HAHN. Does it work?

HEISENBERG. I think so.

HAHN. Show me.

HEISENBERG. This, here, is a fissionable core of uranium-two-three-five, weighing about fifteen or sixteen kilograms, divided between two separate cylinders. Here is a reflector or a tamper, of sorts, of lead, it could be uranium, to prevent the escape of neutrons. The reflector causes the neutrons to bounce back into the core of fissionable material –

HAHN. Thereby reducing the amount of U-two-three-five required.

HEISENBERG. Exactly.

HAHN. Diebner isn't going to like that.

HEISENBERG. Spontaneous fission or cosmic radiation could provide the necessary neutron to start the chain reaction. Better would be an initiator like a tiny sample of radium.

HAHN. I'm impressed. But how is it made to explode at the right moment?

HEISENBERG. Each one of the separate cylinders would be too small to produce an explosion on their own. Once dropped from the aircraft at the chosen altitude, one half would be fired, like a bullet from a gun, at the other half to start the chain reaction. My best estimate suggests that it would only take about ten to the minus-six seconds. Ten to the minus-five on a good day.

HAHN. A thing of technical beauty. And is this what the Americans have done?

HEISENBERG. It's what I'd do.

HAHN. Just because you know the recipe for making an omelette, doesn't mean you can cook a nice one. And I think it unlikely, if we do make it back to Germany, that you'll be allowed to waltz off and produce an atom bomb of your own, but I'm delighted for you if your ego has been appeased. Mostly, however, I'm relieved that it took you till now to work it out.

Silence.

HAHN *is in the doorway when he turns back –*

Heisenberg?

HEISENBERG. Hm?

HAHN. You came up with that all this evening?

HEISENBERG. Yes.

HAHN. All of it?

HEISENBERG. Yes.

HAHN. You hadn't done those calculations before?

HEISENBERG. No.

HAHN. Never before tonight?

HEISENBERG. No.

HAHN. That is very quick.

Scene Fourteen

January 1946.

All the guests. Their suitcases are packed. They are dressed for the cold weather. Each man is holding a flute of champagne.

WEIZSÄCKER. A toast to the new year, I think.

DIEBNER. To the end of our confinement.

HAHN. And a safe journey home.

ALL. A safe journey home.

They drink.

HEISENBERG. To Hahn's Nobel Prize.

DIEBNER. Yes.

VON LAUE. To Hahn.

ALL. To Hahn.

They drink.

WEIZSÄCKER. How does it feel, Hahn?

HAHN. Unbelievable.

HEISENBERG. What was it again? 'Professor Otto Hahn…'?

HAHN. 'Professor Otto Hahn, German radiologist, has been awarded the 1944 Nobel Prize for Chemistry', yadda, yadda, yadda. 'It has been stated in official circles that Otto Hahn has been detained since the end of the year. No further comment was available.'

WEIZSÄCKER. I'd glad someone is still talking and thinking and stating about us. It's reassuring to know that we still matter, even if only in 'official circles'.

BAGGE. How much is a Nobel Prize worth these days?

HEISENBERG. About six thousand pounds, I think.

HAHN. It's not about the money.

BAGGE. Six thousand pounds is, what, about one hundred and twenty thousand marks?

VON LAUE. It's a great honour, Hahn. I can think of no one more deserving.

BAGGE. How much is a pound of sugar?

HEISENBERG. About forty pfennigs.

VON LAUE. Do you think Edith has heard the good news?

HAHN. Oh, I'm sure.

BAGGE. So, if the Nobel Prize was awarded in sugar, Hahn would receive the equivalent of one hundred and fifty thousand kilograms.

VON LAUE. I'll bet she's thrilled.

BAGGE. And if one kilogram of sugar contains about four thousand calories...

HAHN. Edith doesn't care about this sort of thing.

DIEBNER. The pomp and pageantry.

BAGGE. Consequently, the Nobel Prize for Chemistry amounts to... six hundred million calories. There you go, Hahn. Congratulations on your six hundred million calories!

HAHN. Thank you, Bagge.

Pause. They sip their champagne.

WEIZSÄCKER. Will they let you go to Sweden? To collect the prize.

HAHN. I don't know. I'd like to go.

WEIZSÄCKER. And if they ask where you've been the past seven months, what will you tell them?

HAHN. Nothing. Not if Rittner doesn't want me to. I won't say a word.

Beat. WEIZSÄCKER *thinks.*

WEIZSÄCKER. I am so embarrassed. By all of it.

HAHN. So am I.

Silence.

BAGGE. I shall be very relieved to have something to work on again.

DIEBNER. Will we be allowed to? They'll be watching us like hawks. I fear we'll be limited to teaching.

BAGGE. They wouldn't waste us like that, would they?

DIEBNER. I can't bear undergraduates.

BAGGE. I would understand if Diebner and I were somewhat restricted, but not the rest of you.

WEIZSÄCKER. Who would have us?

HAHN. We'll have to wait and see. I worry that nuclear physics will never be a truly clean, open subject again. Right now, I'm sure it has the gleam of something like black magic.

HEISENBERG. I don't need to work on nuclear physics, but I need to work on something.

WEIZSÄCKER. Cosmic rays?

HAHN. Can you work on cosmic rays in Germany? Do we have mountains high enough? You might need to go somewhere else for that.

HEISENBERG. I won't. I stayed in Germany during the war, to be in Germany after the war.

WEIZSÄCKER. I'm going into philosophy.

The sound of a car horn. The guests pick up their suitcases, all but one, and begin to file out the door.

BAGGE. It's a good sign that Rittner will be flying home with us. It suggests they don't intend to kill us off in a plane crash.

The door shuts behind them. Farm Hall is quiet.

Suddenly, HEISENBERG is back. He picks up the forgotten suitcase, turns to leave, but then turns back.

He gazes around the room, then speaks into the empty space –

HEISENBERG. We had been working in a cave in the base of a cliff in Haigerloch. For weeks we had done nothing but slave over this would-be nuclear reactor. This nothing. A heap of graphite in a hole in the ground. One morning, very early, I left Weizsäcker and Bagge asleep in their beds and I went home. I spent ten days with Elisabeth and my children, and then Sam Goudsmit came. He picked me up, took me to Belgium, Versailles, and then you came, Rittner, if you're still listening. I hope you are.

Pause.

You brought me here and I remember feeling very relieved. Something about being here, of all places, felt like a return to form. Truthfully, it felt like being back at the university in Göttingen. The six of us, in our padded world. Nothing to do but sit and talk and argue. I didn't realise how tired I was. Coming here, I felt like an exhausted swimmer, finally setting foot on dry land. I just hope I won't be too tired to get back into the water.

Pause.

Diebner asked: 'What is the truth?' The answer is I don't know. At the best of times, each morning we wake up an entirely different person. Rittner, I have felt like an entirely different person every morning for the past twelve years.

Some mornings I thought, today I will be brave. Today I will do the right thing. But what is the right thing? What's right for me, might not be right for my family. What's right for my work, might not be right for my country. How was I supposed to know what was right? On some mornings I didn't care either way, because my wife was pregnant, or my mother was sick or something else had happened that day that felt more important... I'd lost my keys.

It has only been since coming here that I have felt like myself, like there is one of me again. My realities have converged. I know exactly where I am, and so know nothing about where I'm going.

What is the truth, Rittner? To put the question bluntly: 'Did you try to build a bomb?' Well, on some mornings, yes, and on others, no.

The End.

A Nick Hern Book

Farm Hall first published in Great Britain in 2023 as a paperback original by Nick Hern Books Limited, The Glasshouse, 49 Goldhawk Road, London W12 8QP, in association with Jermyn Street Theatre

Farm Hall copyright © 2023 Katherine Moar

Katherine Moar has asserted her moral right to be identified as the author of this work

Extracts from *Blithe Spirit* by Noël Coward are reproduced by kind permission of Methuen Drama, an imprint of Bloomsbury Publishing Plc

Cover image: Ciaran Walsh

Designed and typeset by Nick Hern Books, London
Printed in the UK by Mimeo Ltd, Huntingdon, Cambridgeshire PE29 6XX

A CIP catalogue record for this book is available from the British Library

ISBN 978 1 83904 217 1

Woodland
CARBON
www.woodlandcarbon.co.uk
NICK HERN BOOKS
Printed on Carbon Captured paper

www.nickhernbooks.co.uk

facebook.com/nickhernbooks

twitter.com/nickhernbooks